Edited by Clementine Burnley
and Sharon Dodua Otoo

W0088777

Winter Shorts

Winter Shorts

edited by Clementine Burnley and Sharon Dodua Otoo

Witnessed - Edition 5

www.witnessed-series.blogspot.com

www.edition-assemblage.de

Editors: Clementine Burnley and Sharon Dodua Otoo

Copy Editing: Laura Barker, Cienna Davis, Alexa Dvorson, Karina Griffith, Zari Harat, Leah King, Gyavira Lasana, Anne Radtke, Polly Tuckett, Bartosz Wójcik and Amy Zamarripa Solis

Cover Illustration: Sita Ngoumou

Proofreading: Clementine Burnley, Sharon Dodua Otoo, Jens Weisbrod and Bartosz Wójcik

Cover Layout: Markus Weiß (www.typogo.de)

Layout: Jens Weisbrod

Printing: CPI Clausen & Bosse, Leck

Printed in Germany 2015

Praise for *Winter Shorts*

"The stories in *Winter Shorts* depict characters who are displaced in many senses: geographically, socially, culturally, linguistically – and, most importantly of all, they are black people in a white world. The winter of the title clearly stands as a metaphor for the cold, alien environment of Germany and Austria in which the characters, and perhaps the authors themselves, are outsiders. The majority of contributors to this volume are appearing in print for the first time. Witnessed is to be congratulated on having supported this project and for having provided this platform for black voices to tell their own stories in their own words."

Máire Davies, Honorary Fellow, Royal Holloway, University of London, United Kingdom

"*Winter Shorts* is a very important collection of writings by African Diasporic/Black writers that turn global white supremacy on its head in both subtle and profound ways. Each contribution reminds this African-American cultural worker that the struggle to define and redefine oneself in countries that consistently marginalize and demonize Blackness is international. Co-Editors Clementine Burnley and Sharon Dodua Otoo did a masterful job with compiling a diverse group of extraordinary authors whose writings defy the myth of the monolithic African/Black experience."

Aishah Shahidah Simmons, Producer/Director, *NO! The Rape Documentary* and Sterling Brown, Visiting Professor of Africana Studies, Williams College, United States and an Associate Editor for *The Feminist Wire*

"*Winter Shorts* gave me feelings similar to those I had when I was a little girl devouring my late paternal grandmother's bookshelf, a space that introduced me to Toni Morrison, Ralph Ellison, Ann Petry, James Baldwin, Gloria Naylor, and other legendary Black writers. It gave me feelings similar to those that I have when I'm with family eating BBQ, drinking cocktails, and playing cards. It gave me feelings similar to those I have when I'm at an academic conference full of Black folk. It gave me feelings similar to those I have when I visit my friends and comrades in Berlin. The feeling is this: I am honored and blessed to be part of such a rich, complex, and electric community full of joy, pain, laughter, sadness, fear, excitement. The misery Burnley caresses in "Boom" is there. The embarrassment that turns into pain that turns into anger is there, as Iroh embraces in "Support a Black-Owned Business Especially at Christmas." The oblivion that Simpson massages in "Raw" is there, too. It's all there, because, as Burnley points out, "The characters in our stories are hurting but they are finding ways to make it on their own terms, without giving up their identities." Although she has transcended this life, Toni Cade Bambara always reminds us that the writer's job is to "make the revolution irresistible." The many brilliant writers who share their voices with us in *Winter Shorts* take up this tremendous task by reminding us that the revolution happens in our hearts, minds, and spirits during moments when we might least expect it."

Dr. Heidi R. Lewis, Assistant Professor of Feminist & Gender Studies, Colorado College, United States and an Associate Editor for *The Feminist Wire*

Contents

Introduction – On Contested Belonging

A Conversation between Clementine Burnley and Sharon Dodua Otoo

> "Our lives are a battlefield on which is fought a continuous war between the forces that are pledged to confirm our humanity and those determined to dismantle it; those who strive to build a protective wall around it, and those who wish to pull it down; those who seek to mould it and those committed to breaking it up; those who aim to open our eyes, to make us see the light and look to tomorrow […] and those who wish to lull us into closing our eyes."

> - Ngugi Wa Thiong'o

SO: This is a beautiful quote to open our conversation. I'd like to think that we both belong to the group of people who aim to open eyes…

CB: I believe we do. I think our edited collection *Winter Shorts* shows us contemporary Germany through the eyes of people who are often seen as peripheral to the cultural mainstream.

SO: Germany *and* Austria!

CB: Yes! And each of the stories illustrates a grappling with definitions of self and belonging. It seems that for the characters in this collection, identity can't be taken for granted. Insteasud, in showing how they see themselves, our characters also fight against false identities imposed by the people around them.

SO: Can you say a bit more about what you mean by that?

CB: I mean that people who happen to be part of the wider African diaspora often come to resist the way in which negative behaviour is racialised, that is, presented as "typical" of African Diasporans. We come to resist the systematic institutional violence against black (deliberately lower-case) people worldwide. In *Winter Shorts* all the authors use their writing to reflect on exactly how Blackness is created. To be part of the wider African diaspora or to be Black, which is not always the same thing, is to see heritage, experience and education as sometimes separate and sometimes the same.

SO: Yes, I completely agree. At least if we are somehow conscious. I definitely see myself as both: I am part of the wider African diaspora and I am Black. And I see the Witnessed book series, of which *Winter Shorts* is part, as a platform where heritage, experience and education – and I would add empowerment – are woven together.

CB: Can you say a little more about the Witnessed Series? What motivated you to start it?

SO: Yes of course. I had been politically active in Germany for around six years already when the idea came. I noticed how, despite well over 300 years of resistance, the dominant German society still perpetuated the idea of a white norm, against which all else was measured. As an activist, I found it extremely frustrating that our voices were rarely heard and were often distorted in the dominant media. That African Diasporans in Germany are rarely called upon to speak as "experts" on current political affairs, and that our protests against various forms of racism, be it the use of blackface, the prevalence of racial profiling or the use of racist vocabulary in children's books, are ignored, trivialised or met with a viciously defensive and un-empathetic backlash. However when we received support from Anglophone countries, we usually made progress.

CB: So the idea to create an English-language book series was born?

SO: Exactly. The series is a platform for other African Diasporans in Germany to testify in English to their experiences here, so that a larger international audience has access to these experiences.
But I would like to ask you something about what you said before. The third book of the Witnessed series is *Daima. Images of Women of Colour in Germany* by our wonderful late friend Nzitu Mawakha. In your contribution to the book you wrote "…I did not grow up Black…" and I have often wondered about that. I have heard of other women who say they only began to identify as Black when they lived in predominantly white contexts. In fact, this is the reason Nzitu chose the subtitle: because although all the women included in the book experienced racist marginalisation, they did not all necessarily identify as "Black". "People of Colour" (also known as PoC) is a term which is still relatively new in Germany. It is inspired by the US-American self-chosen political identity, which builds on the idea of solidarity for all people who are racialised and "othered" in predominantly white societies and respects the fact that within the scope of this umbrella term, different communities experience different forms of racialisation. Of course there are no clear cut boundaries: biologically we are all human beings. But these self-chosen political definitions are used to try to make sense of our lived experience. I have always thought of "Black" (capital letters) as simply a social construct, which I used to describe all African Diasporan people who are racialised, and I never use the word "black" (lower case). Now I wonder if to be "Black" (capital letters) is more of an active choice? If it means to resist being othered? And if to simply be "part of the wider African diaspora" is rather more based on the concept of "belonging"?

CB: When I think about it, perhaps it was more that black (deliberately lower-case) in Cameroon was invisible. There was no "white" alternative, no powerful majority against which to define us as other. We were simply black. We knew about racialisation, we'd heard about slavery and our parents had experienced colonialism. But I would still say we had no political (race) consciousness. Now I realise that racism is simply a way to hide the operation of a brutal white supremacy, which in the post-colonial era continues to violently exploit black labour worldwide. Racism tells us that white supremacy is the "natural order" of things. I reject that way of thinking. So I define Black (with a capital B) as being deliberately race conscious and as resisting othering; whereas being part of the African diaspora is simply being black. Because black people may also resist political race consciousness.

SO: That's really interesting and I now realise it's an aspect I hadn't thought about that much before. In other words, you don't have to be politically Black to have a feeling for being "the other"? I have to think of Muriel Mben's main character, Ugochi Emeka, in "The Unruly Passenger." Ugochi definitely has a strong sense of her African identity and heritage. She makes sure to befriend someone from Benin while she is in university and on a regular basis she visits relatives who can cook Nigerian food for her. I would say that an understanding of being politically Black would have come through the numerous experiences of being othered and of being treated in a hostile manner. Because of this Ugochi Emeka has the ability to second-guess people – she knows how they are likely to see her. And this enables her to triumph at the end of the story.

CB: I think all the writers of *Winter Shorts* are opening windows on Blackness. Sometimes the view out of those windows is familiar to us and sometimes we see something we are not expecting. Which makes sense because while Black people may share many experiences, the personal histories and context in which those experiences occur may be quite different.

SO: Precisely. A lot of the knowledge contained in this book, as well as its presentation in the form of creative writing, may seem unconventional to some. There are a lot of words, phrases, expressions and concepts contained between these pages which are not universally accessible or at least not well represented in dominant cultural and media outlets. But I'm ok with that because I think the moment of confusion and uncertainty is a powerful opportunity to unlearn dominance. And Witnessed is deliberately about centre-ing the Black experience. You know, this whole conversation is reminding me of the concept of "double consciousness" coined by the distinguished African-American sociologist and historian W.E.B. Du Bois.

CB: Yes, me too. Du Bois wrote about the way double consciousness comes into being for us as Black people, because society sees us through a largely negative filter of assumptions and prejudices. Double consciousness is about both aspects: how we see ourselves as individuals or as a group and how society sees us. Some people call this two-ness. I would speak about three-ness because sexuality and gender identity are also important to how I see myself. In Elsa Mbala's "December Rain," the main character has "many versions of herself." She describes this multiplicity beautifully.

SO: I remember having conversations with people, particularly in Germany, who felt the term "double consciousness" was about the feeling of being in the middle – not belonging anywhere really. Like, I grew up in the UK and I have Ghanaian roots. Back then, I never felt really at home in either setting. But the concept of "double consciousness", as Du Bois meant it, has always been fascinating to me. I see this as a talent. Like a superpower. The ability to see yourself from your own perspective and also to see yourself as others see you. These days I am wondering if it is a skill that should only be used sparingly; when I have other people's view of me in my mirror, I find it difficult to move freely, to breathe easily, to laugh authentically. Maybe double consciousness is also a curse? What do you think?

CB: I like the idea of having this superpower but of course I see the difficulties as well. So I have no real answer. I don't know what I really am. That changes all the time. It's a dilemma because while I am really not interested in how society sees me, I have learned that it's unsafe to be read as criminal, terrorist or as hypersexual. Nowadays, people talk about "third culture-kids," about moving between cultures and societies before one has developed a strong sense of one's own identity. Perhaps that's similar to being in the middle? In any case I think that many of us share this feeling of being in-between. My experiences were of growing up in Cameroon and then trying to be accepted in Europe. Trying to be "integrated," which is a concept I don't like very much for the false promises of acceptance it offers to the conforming immigrant. I felt fine in both places, but I constantly had to defend my presence both in Cameroon and in Europe.

SO: Having grown up in the UK and lived in Germany, I understand what you mean about Europe. But you were born and raised in Cameroon. Why did you have to defend your presence there?

CB: In both places people commented on the way I spoke English, on my foreign names, and used those two markers to quickly assign me a place in the class hierarchy. I find class is an important part of my identity. My parents both had university educations and professional jobs, so I am aware of my class privilege. Speaking English fluently gives me a language privilege, and conditions my opposition to systemic marginalization of Anglophones in a de facto "Francophone" state, although we are supposed to be a bilingual country. Not speaking a Cameroonian language fluently reduces my belonging within some Cameroonian circles, although there are many third-culture children in Cameroon. As soon as people from different areas fall in love the chances of their children speaking a Cameroonian language ... well, that chance goes down. What's more troubling is that people question the belonging of my Krio community in Cameroon, because some of my ancestors were enslaved and some returned as missionaries. This kind of ethnic-based nationalism is dangerous wherever it occurs. One hundred and seventy-five years has to be enough time to settle into a place and call it home.

SO: My parents did not attend university. They left Ghana in the 1960s and met by chance and married in London. I definitely grew up marginalised. For example, I didn't speak English when I first started school, I was the only Black child in my class, and I was a girl on top of that! I dealt with sexism at home and racism at school. It was an awkward time and I didn't find a positive identity to my Black womanhood until I was somewhere in my mid-20s. The feeling of not-belonging anywhere was so strong, I decided to make my permanent home in Germany – how much more not-belonging can you get than that?!

CB: Not much more, I think. It's interesting though. The things you do now place you in the mainstream of German culture. Speaking this "not belonging" in German media and culture is a kind of belonging that many Germans will never have.

SO: I am not so sure that I am in the mainstream of German culture. But perhaps I am one of those small exceptions that are allowed – the exceptions, which confirm the rule.

CB: For me it's striking for my ancestors to have been kidnapped to work on white plantations, to return with black and white missionaries and for me still to be fighting for acceptance after five generations. I wonder if anyone belongs anywhere or if it's better just to find a place to stand your ground. We all come from earth, don't we?

SO: I would definitely say it is time to redefine the notion of belonging.

CB: In "December Rain" the main character feels that her spiritual home is in Cameroon but admits to feeling she belongs in every country where she has lived...

SO: This is really a theme that runs through a number of the stories. I am thinking of Anokye in my story "Whtnacig Pnait (Watching Paint)" who just does not feel at home in Germany. And then we have the ladies in Njideka S. Iroh's "Support a Black-Owned Business Especially at Christmas." They love their "village" (Vienna) but they also have *Fernweh* – there's no translation of this into English. It's a kind of homesickness for places which are far away from home.

CB: These characters are not taking much nonsense though. The characters in our stories are hurting but they are finding ways to make it on their own terms, without giving up their identities. I think that I did not hang on so tight to my identity at the beginning. I would have chucked it away to be accepted, but that didn't work. And then I realised that "integration" is a trick. At the end you are stripped naked but may still not be accepted, and you can lose your self-respect and your community in the process.

SO: Yes. Integration is the carrot dangled in front of those with a so-called migration background. It will never be attained but we are told it is what we should be aiming for. We are told to keep chasing that damn carrot! I like the way that the main characters in all the stories are grappling with many issues, but integration is not one of them.

CB: I am still thinking about this idea of a superpower. Well; double consciousness could be like the "Other" talking back. Like the Mona Lisa saying that she was tired of art critics interpreting her smile. On the one hand, we are familiar with the filter of negative assumptions through which society views social "others". We know the stereotypes and we know what "normal" is supposed to look like too. While people with a single consciousness think that the world works the same way for everyone, people with a double consciousness know that it does not. On the other hand, people with single consciousness see no contradiction between how they live and how "others" live. The difference seems to be explained by otherness. Or perhaps they simply do not see the "other" at all. Du Bois calls this "veiling". The "other" is invisible. In the recent US-American film "The Help" it's clear that having maids in the room with you is like having pets. The employers speak without inhibition. Because it doesn't matter what the "help" think. In my short story "Boom" the tourists do not recognise the old man except as a seller or beggar. And that means they cannot interpret the important message he is carrying.

SO: Yes, this is very true. We can also see this in a very explosive way in Tigist H. Schmidt's story "Very Christmassy" – how the Granny reacts to Sarah, someone the Granny considers to be other. And I really love how Noah Hofmann in his story "Winter in Europe" addresses this theme by taking a humorous look at "single consciousness" from the perspective of an African travelling to Europe.

CB: "Winter in Europe" manages to reverse so many stereotypes in a joyfully ironic way. I laughed out loud when I read it. With regard to single consciousness: In "Raw" Tobias notices how his girlfriend Rachel is stared at, or how he and Rachel are stared at when they are together. I don't know if this means he is seeing the world in a different way because normally white people are read as socially dominant worldwide. Can white people acquire the same sensitivity to "othering" as people who are marginalised?

SO: I would like to think so. But I think the reality is, most white people get the sensitivity only when they experience marginalisation themselves. And even then it is not guaranteed when it comes to talking about racism. Tobias noticed it because it affected Rachel, but it also directly affected him: he was stared at too. And then he was able to simply step away from it – he could end the relationship and leave "double consciousness" behind him. That's kind of the definition of white privilege, isn't it?

CB: Ben does something very similar in "Very Christmassy." What he wants is to be loved and accepted the way he is, but he brings his girlfriend unprotected into a very dangerous situation and then ignores her distress.

SO: It's amazing how people will go out of their way to downplay or even deny the existence of racism, right?

CB: Yes. I believe that people invest more effort in denying racism than in dealing with it because facing the purpose for which institutional racism is constructed, is painful. Racism is a rationale to distribute social benefits by ethnicity. So, resisting racism brings members of socially dominant groups into a situation of discomfort for no immediate benefit.

SO: I find it really hard to speak about racism in certain contexts now. It seems to trigger a kind of aggressive-defensiveness that I am no longer ready to deal with. Probably I am not alone.

CB: No, I think you are not. We see this for example in Monique Simpson's "Raw," where Rachel faces the "Where do you come from, really?" conversation. In "December Rain" M'bala puts it well when she describes arguing with lecturers about the importance of intention in deciding what is racist behaviour or speech as the difference: "between well-meant racism and racism."

SO: Oh yes. And this is a moment that all Black people as well as other people of colour understand only too well. Do you remember that moment in my short story "Whtnacig Pnait (Watching Paint)" where Siggi is asking Anokye about his name and Mustafa simply rolls his eyes?

CB: I do. It was completely familiar. White people often play the role of the *Ausländerbehörde* (German immigration control office) and check the extent to which "others" belong to "their" society. Although I think the most difficult conversations for me are those I have with people who consider themselves allies but who charge a price for their ally-ship. These people ignore my experiences, or ask me to pretend that my experience is the same as theirs, or that their experience is more representative than mine. Sometimes they simply require a lot of attention – they cry, they drain, they require gratitude…

SO: Some call it Oppression Olympics...

CB: …people can only do this by ignoring racism in their analysis of sexism, heterosexism and classism. I feel torn when the left ask me to ignore the harms of racism in the struggle for class justice, when feminists ask me to ignore the racism and classism within the white feminist movement; the privilege white women can derive from their preferential access to less exploitative forms of employment, from being married to wealthy, powerful men and from their use of a low-paid racialised domestic labour force. In these conversations I feel more invisible than when I am confronted with really open racism.

SO: And I would argue that we still have a long way to go to dismantle sexist, heterosexist, cissexist and ableist structures in Black communities and Black political organisations too. Even by calling these forms of oppression by their names I feel like I am doing something radical. I should probably define them too, right?

CB: Why not?

SO: Well for me Black spaces still have to work against logics of oppression. Black men need to reflect and work against male privilege every much as straight people need to think about ways that gay, lesbian, bisexual and queer people experience marginalisation and violence (or "heterosexism") in Black communities. Cissexism is a word which describes the way people who are happy with the gender they have been assigned and have never had to question this (cisgender people) are privileged at the cost of those who do not have this experience (for example transmen, transwomen, genderqueer and gender non-conforming among others). And in "Whtnacig Pnait (Watching Paint)" I touch slightly on the question of ableism. Even in a so-called "safe space" for people of colour, Anokye still does not feel completely at ease because of his daily experience of being discriminated against for having a disability (dyslexia). But I have to say, especially in Germany, I am generally far more optimistic about the work that is being done in African-Diasporan contexts on these issues.

CB: Ableism is important and your handling of it is inspiring. Did I say that already? I do think that despite the fact that women and queer people are expected to put their struggles with sexism, cissexism and heterosexism aside in order to support the struggle for racial equality, there is still reason to be cautiously optimistic about the work done in our own spaces. At the same time: We have to guard against the tendency to live against negative stereotypes, leading to respectability politics, which is something it took me a long time to get my head around.

SO: Can you tell me more about what you mean by that?

CB: Sometimes Black people and other people of colour arrange their lives to disprove racial stereotypes. In doing so, they fall into a trap. Both conformity and reaction are poor replacements for living according to one's own vision. This is also why *not* reacting to whiteness is an important strategy in stopping the constant re-centre-ing of whiteness and its forcible injection into Black experiences. Blackness can come to constitute a space that whiteness simply possesses, interprets and consumes. Strangely, we rarely hear white people talk about their race or acknowledge the way in which whiteness itself is constructed as invisible, non-threatening, non-aberrant, normal. Instead most public channels of discussion are filled with stories of dangerous "others". I see the collaborative piece Bino and you have written, "The Romantics and the Criminals," as the Mona Lisa speaking. Especially after the so-called artistic intervention "*Die Toten Kommen*" ("*The Dead are Coming*") where the action-art organisation *Zentrum für politische Schönheit* (Centre for Political Beauty) used the corpses of refugees to shock their audience. The irony is that refugee deaths and the bodies of people of colour are once more instrumentalised and dehumanised using kitsch horror techniques. The bodies of Black people and other people of colour are spoken for, are made sites for unproblematic consumption by white artists and a white public who ignore the continuity of this kind of pseudo-shock action with the *Völkerschau* (human zoo). Dead "others" are accessories to a white experience of perfectly safe transgression of social norms.

SO: We've used the term "people of colour" several times now. I know that this is a contested term in Germany, but I prefer it far more to the term "person with a migration background," which is more common here. The phrase "person with a migration background" seems to suggest that you can see or hear whether a person is of "foreign" descent or not. However "person with a migration background" is a euphemism. It is rarely used to describe certain white non-Germans – I think white US Americans for example do not feel addressed by it. On the other hand, people who were born and raised in Germany, and who do not look white, are often labelled as having a "migration background." Well I did migrate to Germany – I come from the UK. But dominant German society does not have this in mind when my migration background becomes of relevance. My white friend, who also comes from the UK, will always either fit in as German (at first sight) or be welcomed to German society as a fellow European. My bilingual Berlin-born children are spoken of as having a "migration background", a description which to date has not been bestowed upon my friend's white bilingual Berlin-born son.

CB: When people with dark skin, or with dark hair and eyes cross borders, their expectations are … different. The queues they stand in take longer to inspect. Their papers are scrutinised more thoroughly. An Afro-German with light-skin privilege described to me how on a train from Florence to Munich she saw dark-skinned people or people with "Middle Eastern features" being singled out for identity checks and being shouted at or physically mishandled during these identity checks. Although she is Black she was not asked to show her identification. A very specific type of racial profiling frequently takes place on the borders between Italy and Germany. Dark-skinned, dark-haired people heading for a chance at a future are read as "criminal." Although until a hundred years ago there were no passports at all. Europeans escaping from poverty and war managed to occupy Australia, North and South America and to control large parts of Africa. European capital and European consumption help to drive systematic economic exploitation that influences migration flows worldwide. Europeans continue to travel wherever they please in the world but most Europeans do not recognise their freedom to cross borders for luxury travel as a privilege. They see themselves as completely different from fellow humans who are being stopped and treated very badly for trying to exercise the same freedom - not just for holidays but also for their survival.

SO: Kind of like the experience of Muriel Mben's main character in "The Unruly Passenger"? Ugochi Emeka was looked at in a degrading way by a fellow train passenger who did not want her to sit next to him. He also racially profiled her, I would say.

CB: Yes. When a white person sees someone being racially profiled, what happens inside them? I can't say. I know that I feel as if the person being profiled could be me. So I feel I should do something. I have had conversations with security and with airline staff on both Air France and SN Brussels about my discomfort at a fellow passenger being physically restrained, screaming and being forced to remain in his seat. I tell them that I have read of people being killed by the sort of physical restraint they are applying. On one particular Air France flight, the plane takes off anyway while a man is screaming his lungs out. It takes 90 minutes to calm him down. Afterwards the security guards changed into Air France uniforms and served us drinks and food. Only a few of the Black passengers seemed concerned about the man's welfare and most of them are resigned to these incidents. The white passengers all pretended the deportee did not exist. I suppose that I identified with the deportee and perhaps the white passengers identified with the immigration and security? The only thing that made an impression on the Air France staff is when I constructed myself as a dissatisfied customer who was being traumatised by the noise. Otherwise the staff simply laughed in my face. As if human distress does not matter.

SO: And this is how Black people are dehumanised. The only way your protest, Clementine, is taken seriously is if you pose a financial threat. Interestingly, in your story "Boom," this kind of arrogance ended up having serious consequences for the main characters. If Anke and Mimi had taken the old man seriously, they would have perhaps tried a little more sincerely to find out what exactly he wanted to tell them. It actually wasn't all that difficult to understand.

CB: To Anke and Mimi the old man cannot possess anything which is important. They do not read him as a producer of knowledge. They assume he is asking rich tourists for something.

SO: And I am also reminded of the character Hermann in "Lichterfelde Blues." His arrogance is on a similar level, isn't it? He displays an utter disregard for Idris and the main character in your short story. It does not occur to him that he should show the common respect he would no doubt show to white neighbours.

CB: Yes, he probably would. However, the characters in "Lichterfelde Blues" resist Hermann's assumptions and actions. I do think that identity can be situated, contextual and shifting. I see it as quite slippery. We can fight for our identity. For instance, an important theme for a few stories in this collection is gender identity. Or rather how we see ourselves as gendered, un-gendered, or gender-fluid.

SO: I think I see this the most clearly in WoMANtís RANDom's story "Waste of Mist."

CB: The way we read gender comes up in Noah Hofmann's story "Winter in Europe" too. Hofmann removes the familiar language we are used to when we describe male and female, masculine and feminine and leaves us struggling to see something that isn't so easily classified or assigned value based on that classification.

SO: True. As a cis-woman I have a very limited perspective on gender fluidity. Here I clearly see my role as stepping to one side and leaving the stage for gender-gifted people. Of course, it is up to those people ultimately if they want to take that stage or not. Or if they want to build their own stages – and my role would be to amplify those. And to sit down and listen. I am really honoured therefore that WoMANtís RANDom did agree to share their creativity with us. Our collection is all the richer for it. And I love the humour of "Winter in Europe"!

CB: What we think gay, or gender non-conforming or queer, or out are, is quite dominated by white visions of rainbows and kiss-ins. Public declaration, signalling through dress and behaviour – all these things are coded in different ways in different cultures. I would love to see more visions of PoC and Black queerness. As writers we have this ability to stand a little bit apart from what we experience, to observe and analyze. This is both a gift and a responsibility. It's up to us whether we use our two-ness or three-ness or many-ness for our collective sustenance, as the source of abundance, joy and freedom.

SO: I think you sum it up well. It is both: a gift and a responsibility.

CB: The stories in this collection are the result of these kinds of active creative processes.

SO: I really enjoyed the process of putting these stories together. Of working with the authors on their stories. Of working with you as a co-editor. I have very fond memories of the Skype conversations we had with many of the authors in May. Of discussions about our work, our visions, our hopes. I think we managed to centre our creativity during that time. Something that I guess Black people all over the world could be doing much more of?

CB: Perhaps it's something that Black people could be shown to do more of, since we are creating with words all the time. In Black communities there are great storytellers and orators. Black speech rhythms are very often poetic. The Celts have their bards; Africans have their *griots*. I think the oral traditions of many Black communities can be a resource for our writing. It's definitely better than being spoken for.

SO: Recently, I was invited to participate in a panel discussion called "Can art save the world?" And when I think about how Black people are being dehumanised, my honest answer is: it is the only thing left that can. Hmm... why do I say that?

CB: Maybe because only the unlikely and miraculous can...I think imagination and the repeated description of experience are the only way to reject the kind of totalising white consciousness that tries to redefine what is the actual lived experience of other human beings. Our writers have transformed everyday experiences of being Black, German-speaking, gender-conforming, gender-performing and gender-resisting into reflections on shared struggle, pleasure and inspiration. In her pioneering essay, 'Can the Subaltern Speak?', the critical theorist Gayatri Spivak posed a question about speaking from beyond the margin. Speaking is the act that constitutes a subject, while objects are merely spoken for and spoken about. At least this is how I understand this very complicated concept of subalternity. In speaking, the subaltern escapes the margin for the stage and is no longer spoken by others. Most of the global population is subaltern. Those people have something to say too. As the queer writer and poet Audre Lorde puts it in *Sister Outsider*: "Your silence will not protect you".

SO: No it definitely will not. It may buy us time, but in the end our collective liberation depends on us sharing our stories. All of them!

CB: Very true. The Nigerian novelist Chimamanda Ngozi Adichie has warned us of the danger of a single story, and the American novelist Toni Morrison has told us, "If there's a book that you want to read, but it hasn't been written yet, then you must write it." It is a profound privilege to be part of this collective effort.

The Unruly Passenger

Muriel Mben

Ugochi Emeka entered the train in Frankfurt. She was on her way back home after wandering through *Frankfurter* shops where she had bought winter clothes and white chocolate. She likes to eat all kinds of chocolate, most especially white chocolate. Indeed, she has decided for the umpteenth time to stop consuming it, and has persuaded herself she can stop whenever she wants, but she knows herself that it's a lie; it's her weakness; her addiction. She always has an excuse. This time: she has had a bad day and chocolate will help her to calm down.

While walking through the train, she cautiously checked in her bag to see if she had the train ticket but accidentally pulled her resident permit out, dropping it onto the floor. Frowning her face, she grumbled a "mmh." Annoyed, she looked at the card on the clean and gray floor. "Gray is a sad and ugly color," she thought, while picking up her ID card. She read her name. Her grandma was also called Ugochi. That was a tradition – each girl in the family was named Ugochi. But the tradition changed after the death of three of her female cousins. It was said that "Ugochi" could be a cursed name. To reverse the fortune, Ugochi Emeka decided to be called differently. She was no longer to be referred to as Ugochi, but as "Ugochi Emeka". Her youngest sister did the same. She named herself "Chimi Ugochi." Putting her ID card back inside her bag, Ugochi Emeka continued to look for a seat.

As usual, the clothes Ugochi Emeka was wearing had been selected very carefully: a blue pair of trousers with a yellow pullover. She had tied a tiny yellow scarf around her neck. Though her outfit was beautiful, it was really designed for warmer temperatures. But thanks to her sister Chimi Ugochi who was always "borrowing" her clothes, Ugochi Emeka hardly had anything else left in her wardrobe. It was earlier that morning, while going to her office that she had spontaneously decided to travel to Frankfurt to buy some warm clothes to protect her against the coldness. She hated winter. The landscape reminded her of a horror film. With snow on their branches, the leafless trees around her looked like ghosts. Moreover the gray sky and the coldness always made her feel sad. She had been in Germany for eight years, but she still couldn't get used to the weather.

The first wagon of the train back home was full of silent people who were staring at their mobile phones, while others were reading or sleeping. Ugochi Emeka did not want to go on to the other wagons to check if there were empty seats. Fortunately, she found one seat next to a man with very low cut hair. He smelled of alcohol. She closed her nostrils for a while and asked him if the place was free: of course it was! But she always asked – just in case. The man cast a disdainful look at her as if she was worthless. He turned his head back to the window, shook his head, looked at her one more time and said: "you can sit elsewhere." This disdain moved her but what could she do? Slap him? Mh, bad idea. Or shout? Maybe? She felt small and powerless. She didn't know how to handle the situation and it made her feel more powerless. She remembered how she had been treated by the saleswoman earlier that afternoon and had the unpleasant sensation of being nothing. She experienced a rapid series of emotions. First of all she was angry. She thought: she should have told her mind to that arrogant person in the shop! And now this man! In the shop where she had been nothing but a potential thief and now she was being treated like a *persona non grata*. Secondly, she was annoyed. What gave these people the right to treat her that way? Was she too worthless to sit close to him? He didn't have the right to refuse her the seat. Thirdly, she wanted to cry and to shout her frustration. But she decided to stay polite and replied: "Thanks for your uninteresting answer. Just don't forget to get yourself a personal car." Yeah, yeah she had promised to stay polite but she could not take it. She had to defend herself. What did he think? Was he better than her? She went on to the next wagon.

This one was almost empty. Ugochi Emeka had a free choice of where to sit. She even had a place for her heavy bag, which she threw on the seat. Nobody would give her a bad glance. This idea comforted her. "At least no one will disturb me here!" She said to herself, sitting down. Two minutes later, she took a look inside her shopping bag and grinned. The sight of her clothes – and especially of her chocolate – pleased her. She was calm and forgot her earlier troubles. She was happy about her purchases. Her two pairs of boots and her many colorful scarves and pullovers would last until the next visit of Chimi Ugochi.

When she arrived in Germany, Ugochi Emeka had been a shy girl. Before this time she had lived in Nigeria with her grandmother. Her parents were often on business trips somewhere around the world and they only provided for her material needs. Her grandma took care of her and of her little sister Chimi Ugochi, who was five years younger than her. Chimi Ugochi was the opposite of Ugochi Emeka. She was so innocent, confident and funny! It was always a pleasure having her around. She had many friends and could very easily get in touch with people. Chimi Ugochi only needed to meet someone to talk about everything possible with this person: the weather, politics, her last visit to the dentist or about her boyfriend being unfaithful to her – she had no taboos. She also knew how to get what she wanted from people: Ugochi Emeka could not refuse her anything.

Ugochi Emeka's phone rang when she wanted to take the purchases out of her bag. It was her best friend Afiavi. They first met at university. After her German classes in Hamburg, Ugochi Emeka got a place to study business administration in Giessen. At that time she was young, she was confident and was not prepared for real life. She had had no contact with Germans. She was always hanging out with other foreign students at the language school. Everything and everybody was nice. So, when she arrived at the university she was shocked. She did not expect so much coldness from the people. They were walking in the corridors like robots, looking straight ahead and not paying attention to anything else but their personal goals. Nobody smiled or greeted another unless they were old acquaintances. She felt as if she were invisible. It was very difficult not to cry at the end of the day, when she had faced these closed and inexpressive faces. She remembered wanting to go back to Nigeria. So when she entered the classroom, she almost ran to Afiavi. They were the only two blacks in the classroom. They introduced themselves to each other and stayed together till they finished university. It did not matter that they were from different countries. Afiavi came from Benin. Still they did everything together. They were so close that they introduced each other to their respective families and supported each other during their stay in Germany. Afiavi was now living in Aachen with her husband. After they completed their studies at the university, they stayed in touch and continued to call each other daily for some minutes. They used to talk about their day and about everything else.

Ugochi Emeka did not feel well as she answered the phone. Her encounter with the man and that woman was still disturbing her. She was somehow tired of cold and hostile people and of psychologically fighting to remain strong. She needed happiness and peace. She sometimes wanted to slap some of these people! They had to know that life was beautiful and everything was worth it. Afiavi could hear something was wrong and wanted to know what was bothering her friend.

"It is a long story that needs to be told from the beginning," the young woman replied. Ugochi Emeka started to tell her friend about how everything had started that morning in Giessen.

***

On her way to the bus stop that morning, she had tried to find her way through the thick layer of snow. It was not easy for her, because she was afraid to fall and knowing that the bus would be late, she had not hurried, but taken her time. She had cursed the rotary snow plough for its delay and wished she had a car. Now she had to wait till the bus driver found his way up through the un-cleared snow. Some people were already waiting for the bus when Ugochi Emeka had arrived at the bus station. Standing aside, she had looked into the sad sky then taken her phone to check if she had received a message. No. She had put the phone back in her bag and observed the houses around her. There was nothing to see but snow. Smoke was going out from some chimneys and disappearing into the clouded sky.

Time was going on. Five minutes, ten.... She was about crying. She waited for the bus for so long that her feet started freezing. She could not move them and did not insist on doing so as she noticed they were hardening. Ugochi Emeka felt the biting cold outside. Desperately, without thinking further she decided to go to Frankfurt to buy warmer clothes. She had been planning it for weeks but had not made it. She could no longer postpone her trip even though she had a lot of work to do. That morning, Ugochi Emeka had an appointment at her office in Giessen, with her friend Yacine. They were not really friends or even close. As students, they used to live in the same floor of the same building, but, unlike with Afiavi, Ugochi Emeka and Yacine barely met each other. However Yacine now needed her help and had not hesitated to contact her. Ugochi Emeka disliked to be solicited by people from whom she had not heard for a while. Yacine was looking for another flat. "How the hell did she know I could help her?" Ugochi Emeka thought. Her not-really friend explained to Ugochi Emeka on the phone that she had received a letter of eviction. She had three days to find another room.

Now Ugochi Emeka was shaking. "It is so cold!!!" She almost cried. Her scarf did not keep her warm. Ugochi Emeka still felt the biting cold outside. She should really go to Frankfurt. To remain calm, she started singing in her head: "Oh Frankfurt, a nice place to be!" She has always imagined that town as a mystical place where everything was so clean and chic that she felt at some points that she didn't belong there. Frankfurt was made for rich people. "You just had to look at the big buildings!! They gave you the feeling you were in "New York!" People also dressed up especially in the commercial side of Frankfurt so that you could not guess who was really a big person. No you couldn't. With their sunglasses on, women looked like famous musicians or like American actors. And men all seemed to be important business people with their suits.

Ugochi Emeka looked around her. People seemed worried. They looked from time to time in the direction from where the bus should arrive. She could see that the crowd around her was really upset. "Where is the bus?!" Ugochi Emeka wanted to scream. Powerless, the young woman continued thinking:

"I can't take it anymore. My feet are hurting!" As she was complaining, she saw a woman going up and down. She was talking to herself. Apart from Ugochi Emeka, nobody was paying attention to her. She has always admired that German reserve when it came to other human beings' problems. One day, Ugochi Emeka had a suitcase that was so heavy that she couldn't walk. She needed some help to carry it, but no one stopped to help her. Some other time, an old woman entered the bus and nobody offered her a seat. Since then Ugochi Emeka has known she should only count on herself. Some people say of Germans that they are shy but sometimes she found some of them as cold as winter.

Her friends told her she was wrong. They have had wonderful experiences in Germany. One person related to her that a German family offered her a room in their apartment when she was in need. Another one told her about an old man who spontaneously showed him his way when he went for a job interview in Eschborn. Maybe she had just had bad experiences. But Ugochi Emeka's friends were somehow right. She also had a few German friends whom she could count on. How could she be so hard and forget about it? Nobody is perfect. She should calm down. She was only sad to notice that she had lost her spontaneity after so many years in Germany. She had learned to turn her gaze away when someone smiled at her or when an old woman had no seat in the bus. She also decided to ignore that woman who roved up and down, talking to herself. She had her own problems to put up with.

Turning her face away, Ugochi Emeka touched her scarf. It seemed to be getting thinner and thinner. She could feel the wind hitting her neck as she rearranged the scarf. It was useless. "mmh" she sighed. She wanted to go home to take another one. Which one would she take? She abandoned the possibility of returning home when she heard the bus coming. It was too late. She would be late for her appointment with Yacine if she missed the bus.

Ugochi Emeka led her own estate agency in Giessen. She fought hard to open it after completing her studies. It was not that easy but she stayed focused to achieve her dreams. Some friends and her family had tried to discourage her, but with the help of her husband she made it. The main argument was: "you are black. Do you think THEY would let you open your business?" She always answered with the same words: "How would I figure it out if I don't try? I am the master of my life. I should not allow anyone else to decide for me." Today her name was well-known in the business and people trusted her. She had four employees, whom she recruited as her business grew.

Yacine arrived at the office with ten minutes delay. Ugochi Emeka noticed that she had not changed. She was still slim and so neat. The beauty of her dreadlocks gave Ugochi Emeka the desire to have the same hairstyle. She had not done her hair for a few weeks. She has only been wearing a little acrylic bonnet to protect her hair from the cold temperature. She had struggled so hard to get it to grow that long. Now that she had long hair, she took care of it as she would of her babies. Her husband appreciated her choice of not straightening it. He loved its curly and thick texture. She was happy because he did not belong to the category of African men who wanted black women to relax their hair or to wear weaves. Since she knew that she could get cancer because of relaxers she decided not to do it anymore. She was satisfied with her choice.

Taking care of her tufts of hair and living with it was difficult at the beginning. She hated herself because she felt ugly and so different. Every woman around her, in the media was so beautiful with their weaves, but she resisted. She had entered a new world where she had to learn how to be beautiful with her natural hair. That's why she had created a special file on her computer to collect care methods, pictures of hairstyles and videos of black women who shared their experience about their hair being natural. Ugochi Emeka also had to fight the negative judgment of others. Neither her mother nor her sister understood her choice. But she had met other women in forums and in blogs who discussed about their own experiences. People were not used to seeing a black woman wearing nothing but her natural hair. It was something new for them. So she was sometimes asked: "Won't you do your hair?" or "Will you go out like that?"

"Yes" was her only answer.

She remembered her neighbor spying at her hair in the bus. Once a friend told her she should straighten her hair, she was no longer a baby to keep it natural. "A real woman takes care of her hair. You look like nothing. Please listen to me." Those remarks were sometimes so mean! Besides they looked as though they were really concerned. At some point, Ugochi Emeka had stopped listening to her so-called "good advisers". After all, it was her own head.

So Ugochi Emeka complimented Yacine's hair while they entered her office. After looking at different options, Ugochi Emeka gave Yacine some addresses where she could find apartments in Giessen. They were not really in the centre but were affordable. She could have three rooms, a bathroom and a balcony for 500 euros.

When Yacine had gone one hour later, Ugochi Emeka remembered the coldness of that morning at the bus station. She wondered whether she could have prevented it. What was she thinking when she took a tiny scarf? "Huh." I had forgotten that Chimi took my favorite scarf last time she came home. "*Snief*!!!"

Her sister did not care that Ugochi Emeka only had few bonnets and a single pair of winter boots. She took them all. They had lent each other clothes since their adolescence. Ugochi Emeka had hoped it would have stopped now that they were adults but her sister did not bother at all. Whenever Chimi visited her, she went back home with some of her sister's clothes. Shaking her head, she stood and left for Frankfurt as soon as she had informed her assistant of her planned absence.

Ugochi Emeka did not take long in the shops in Frankfurt. Actually she had only visited two of them. She didn't take time to look at each piece of clothing. She knew exactly what she wanted and refused to get distracted with other things. "In this country you have to be careful with your money. It goes out like rabbits, but it comes back like snails". She couldn't remember who said it but she totally agreed. In fact she also did not want to lose her time. The time she was spending there could have been used for other things. No, shopping was not her favorite activity.

When she entered the first shop, she greeted the saleswoman who did not answer her. Ugochi Emeka felt something like a pinch inside her heart. "Why is she ignoring my greetings?" She tried to disregard it and went inside the shop. She stopped in front of colorful scarves which recalled a rainbow. The young woman touched one green scarf. While contemplating the object of her choice to see if it suited her, she had the bad feeling that she was being observed. From the corner of her eyes, she saw the impolite saleswoman on the opposite side. She seemed to be arranging some clothes. Ugochi Emeka put the scarf back and continued to the next row. A nice blue scarf was calling for her attention. She tested the quality of the material to feel if it was warm enough. "Cotton is always good". She decided to see how it looked like on her and turned it around her neck. For the second time, she had the sensation of being observed. The saleswoman was still arranging some untidy clothes on the opposite side. She got upset.

"I can't believe it!" Ugochi Emeka thought to herself. "She is checking if I am going to steal some articles! Unbelievable!" To see if she was right, the young woman walked to the mirror which was at the end of the shop. She could clearly see the saleswoman going forward as she was moving to the mirror. Ugochi Emeka stopped abruptly and stared at her. The poor saleswoman also stopped, confused. She turned around rapidly and grabbed underwear. Ugochi Emeka burst out laughing and remained quiet. She left the beautiful scarf and went out. She could not accept to be treated like a thief. She went out without a word and without looking at that foolish woman. She did not deserve Ugochi's consideration.

She entered the next shop in the shopping center. She was upset and chose the first clothes she found beautiful. She did not check if they suited her. She was no longer enjoying the experience. She only wanted to go back home. A train would go soon. She hurried up and rushed to the cash desk. The smiling face of the salesman almost calmed her. He was very nice with her. She greeted him politely and went away. She only had fifteen minutes to catch her train. She jumped into the suburban railway. Two stations later, she was at the central train station of Frankfurt. Passing through the black suited crowd, she thought "ohh how sad, I declare black as the official winter colour. As if winter was not sad enough! People should wear colorful clothes in winter". Smiling, she entered the red train on track 16.

***

Ugochi Emeka was now sitting comfortably in the train and talking with her friend on the phone. She started telling Afiavi about her boots.

"Now listen to the story. Do not laugh o, please. You know me. There are always crazy things which happen in my life. You know my favourite boots na, you always laughed at them. You were right oh. Those shoes almost killed me this morning."

"But Ugochi, you only have one pair of shoes?" Her friend Afiavi asked.

"Haha. You know how generous I am with my little sister. She has taken EVERYTHING in my wardrobe. We look physically alike and she takes full advantage of it. Since I am the one working, I have to take care of her."

"I see my sister, go ahead. So you only have those boots."

She said annoyed: "Sister, do not pretend you don't know it. I told you how crazy I was about them! Their brown color and the fur at the top were so nice!!" Ugochi Emeka breathed and paused. She changed the subject of discussion. "This week was very painful for me. It has been snowing for two days now. You know the temperatures are lower when it snows. Today it was freezing and I wore my shoes without any socks."

"Yes, how could you? You told me the shoes are tight…"

"Let me finish *naaa massa*." Her voice rose as she asked Afiavi to wait till the end of the story.

At that same moment a woman sitting nearby in their wagon glanced at her, for a few seconds. Ugochi Emeka stared at her. The old woman seemed irritated by her phone call. Ugochi just didn't bother. She would not want to hang up with her friend because of her. She thought: "Just jump out of the train if you want. It is your problem if you are unhappy about my telephone conversation. I have some joy in my heart and I am expressing it. *Tsuip*." Ugochi Emeka laughed. The old woman looked at her one more time then continued reading her book. She raised it to her face but it seemed she could not concentrate. Then, the old woman closed and laid her book on the empty seat next to her. She crossed her arms and looked outside. She could appreciate the beauty of the white landscape. Ugochi Emeka was still talking with her friend and told her about the old woman in the train. She was really annoyed. Was there any law that prohibited talking inside trains? Ugochi Emeka wondered why some people transferred their frustration on others. She refused to interpret it as racism. It was just too easy. There was surely another explanation. That was not the first time that she had felt stressed on public transportation. The other day a bus driver asked her friends and her to keep quiet although the entire bus was noisy. Why had he decided to pick on them? She could not understand it. Had he addressed them because he thought they could not defend themselves? But she refused to be silenced. The driver had stopped the bus just to control them, and this made her even angrier. They had their tickets. He asked them to get off. "Why?" Everybody watched as she shouted loud in the bus. The big man was afraid and returned to his place. She won. Ugochi Emeka would also win against the old woman that day if the latter would not stop staring at her. She would not accept to be looked upon as if she had done something wrong.

Ugochi Emeka talked for a few more minutes, but eventually they hung up because Afiavi had a visitor. Ugochi Emeka took out her wallet from her bag. She picked something out of it and walked towards the woman. Calmly, Ugochi Emeka stopped next to her and observed her for one or two seconds. Then she handed the old woman a photograph with the words: "I have seen you cannot resist looking at me. Please accept this picture. I would be sorry if you got a stiff neck from constantly looking back towards me." The woman did not laugh at Ugochi Emeka's joke. She looked her up and down and, without answering, stared back at the window. Ugochi Emeka could see the lady had some grey hair. Ugochi's mother once advised her to respect old people but the young woman had come to the conclusion that respect should be reciprocal. She could not respect someone who did not have any consideration for her. Actually already a few years earlier she had decided that she would no longer be affected by those stupid considerations of being rejected or accepted. She had understood how negative thoughts could ruin her life. What she really needed was to concentrate on herself. That strategy was very helpful, and it increased her strength. But she also discovered that she was more irascible in winter. The sad climate stressed her. It was the only time in the year when she continuously felt sleepy. To overcome it she drank a lot of vitamins, ate fruits and visited her sister in France. Those annual visits always invigorated her body and her soul. She became accidentally aware of those techniques. During her first year in Germany she decided to visit her aunt in Belgium. She spent two weeks there hanging with family members and acquaintances. She was happy to speak English. She could fluently express her ideas. It was wonderful not having to worry about the place of the verb in the sentence. She enjoyed it. Her aunt took good care of her. She did not have to worry about anything. Ugochi Emeka ate the Nigerian food that was cooked for her. She did not stay at home, but accompanied her aunt everywhere. Her happiness gave her the strength after her return, to not be broken by the hardness of life. Since then she adopted that strategy.

She sat back at her place, looked through her new scarfs and boots and took out a transparent plastic bag. She was hungry. The noise of the plastic bag caught the attention of the old woman who looked at Ugochi Emeka once more. This time, she did not pay attention to the bitter old woman and was enjoying her food. Some minutes later, a train inspector arrived. He greeted the passengers and checked their tickets. The wagon was not full so he was soon at the old woman's place. He spent more time with her. She was murmuring something and pointed her finger at Ugochi Emeka. Tired of waiting for him, the young woman decided to go to the toilets. She could not take it any longer. As she was heading to the toilets, she noticed that the inspector started following her. She entered the room and took her time. She knew the man was waiting for her outside. She wanted to play. They were approaching Giessen. The young woman moved rapidly to flee the wagon. The train inspector ran after her and she started also to run. She smiled. Some passengers were astonished. They surely wondered what was going on. Maybe they were thinking: "Hasn't that African woman gotten a valid train ticket?" The inspector stopped for two minutes and talked in the phone, and when he had finished he resumed his pursuit. She waited for him. Soon they reached the last wagon. They were arriving in Giessen. Out of breath he asked for her ticket. She just handed him the small piece of paper. He considered her. She could see a mixture of surprise, of reproach, and of anger in his eyes. If he was not worried about the confession of the old passenger, his first questions would have been: "why?"

He opened the door. Policemen were waiting for her. They searched and interrogated her and asked for the drugs. "What drugs?" she asked. The old woman had told the train inspector she was consuming drugs! "Unbelievable!" She opened her bag and got out all the stuff she had bought, placed them on the floor and gave them the plastic bag. The policemen were surprised to discover that she was only eating white chocolate! She liked to break it in small pieces so that she could easily eat it. As the old woman approached them with a smile of victory on her face, she heard the policemen apologizing for their mistake and offering to bring her back home, but Ugochi Emeka refused. As she left, she could see the officers and the inspector approaching the old woman. Ugochi Emeka smiled. The day was rich in emotion, and she needed to rest. As she walked away from the train station, she remembered her misfortunes. Ugochi Emeka was somehow proud of her audacity. However, she would not do it anymore.

December Rain

Elsa M'Bala

She woke up to the gentle sound of water-drops falling against the ceiling and windows. Yes, it was raining, again. She stayed still for a bit, stretched out on the futon. In the nondescript darkness of this closed space, she could have been anywhere in the world. But no time for dreamers, there were things to do, people to call and emails to answer. She pulled herself up and opened the balcony door. The fresh air and the grey morning light harassed her sleepy eyes. The trees had lost most of their leaves but the view was colorful. In the horizon there was pasturage tinted in yellow, green and dark green hues, framed by a surrounding landscape of buildings, like a pistil in its late years.

It was raining in Pforzheim as it did two years ago, the last time she was in Germany. Different corner, similar struggle. Two years ago, further up north, in the city of the free-minded international scholars, rich elderly fur-wearing conservatives and rainy Sundays. Münster perfectly reflected a contradiction from within, its peculiarly arranged gardens and antic churches with the diversity of its rather wild music festivities. Such as the Hawerkamp Festival, where you could switch between a heavy metal crowd and a dancehall/dub step get-down without leaving the building. But what she liked most in that town was her old house. It was a witch-like, two-floor cabana with changing scents, built mostly out of wood. It had survived two world wars and countless attempts by the city to tear it down. It had a Japanese tree garden at the back and was located in the midst of the Aasee Park, five minutes both to her university and to the center of the city and – on top of that – it was affordable! If it wasn't for the mental institution next door, it would have been a keeper. Every Saturday and Sunday one of the neighbors would scream Nazi songs and slogans out his window. It remained a quite frightening experience but, like with everything here, she just got used to it. Plus, she already had a lot on her plate, for example constantly having to debate with her mostly white scholars and professors about the unexciting nuance between well-meant racism and racism. Nevertheless this was home, a place she could always come back to. In winter it was freezing cold, as it was in summer, but the view was golden all year around.

Lutzo was a male street cat that the house adopted years ago. He came and left as he pleased. Even after her roommates had him castrated, he stayed faithful. She often had unpleasant daydreams about ending her life just like that, in an old house with street cats as her only comrades. When she finally had the whole house to herself, her days would consist of watching Spanish cartoons, eating porridge, listening to loud online radio and dancing whenever possible. She loved to watch her locks jump up and down her face, reflecting so much of her, but so little of what her parents saw in her.

"Dreadlocks are just not appropriate for a young intelligent girl like yourself," repeated her mother whenever possible. Eventually though, her mother got used to it. Secretly, she prayed God would help her see her daughter's inner-worth shine brightly. Within these walls, she had successfully created a world within worlds that refused to acknowledge her multifaceted existence. Here she felt comfortable. Others would often peek in, but never stay for long. She always ended up pulling them away, maybe she was afraid that they might get too familiar and she would never be able to enjoy her solitude the way she did now.

She sneezed herself back into this reality. It was cold, but not as cold as she had expected it to be at this time of year. The snow was missing. People had been preparing for the ice – children had carried their sledges out of the basement, parents had their cars pimped out with the best winter tires from the *Stiftung Warentest* ranking list. The expectations were high, as were the disappointments.

She suddenly remembered the very first time she saw those solid water drops falling from the sky. She was eleven when she arrived from Cameroon with little baggage, her two brothers and her mother in the heat of the August sun in south Germany. Her mother had realized the impossible: after years of studying in a foreign language, working for minimal pay and saving whatever was possible, she had brought her three children to Europe, all by herself. From then on, it was the longest countdown to winter. Such a wonderful time! Children got a lot of gifts, ate all the candy they wanted and watched the Americanized versions of this cheerful time on television. Basically like in Yaoundé but with one major difference, there was sugar powdery dust falling from the sky. A friend at Toussaint Antoine primary school in Yaoundé confirmed that the white man is closer to God simply because of that fact. Therefore she considered it an honor to be the first one of her girlfriends who could see, touch and play with this magical element that they only knew from television. It was watery and tasteless.

She decided to start that morning with the most dreadful task of all: what is the goal of you returning to Cameroon? She had been writing and researching for this innovative project, she could only launch there, yet was still unable to face her family or friends with a satisfying answer. As she didn't have one herself, she needed to be there, see and smell that city again, the one she now had vanishing memories of. She had spent the last few years traveling and learning about various places, outside the realms of an academic institution. For most people it was not worth a thing, yet for her it was the best way to encounter the unwritten, the unknown.

"You need to have your qualifications straight here, not experiences! As long as you were not granted a certificate by a well-acclaimed professor with award-winning professional methods, it does not count!"

That voice, again. After her baccalaureate, she took a break from school, officially to figure out what she wanted to do with her life. Unofficially, she felt confused that she was being asked to decide what she was going to do for the rest of her life at eighteen years of age. So during the following two years she traveled throughout Europe. After her Bachelor degree she took another two-year break that led her to America, the Caribbean and Cameroon. And everywhere she landed she felt as if a part of her had always belonged there. She easily connected to places and their stories, but hardly with their citizens. She liked to remember how her grandmother in Cameroon used to groan to herself. She didn't like what the white man's school was doing to her children, always reinterpreting and analyzing one's words. Would the doctor have taken better care of her, especially during her last years, if she had spoken more in French? Right up until her death three years ago, her grandmother did understand but wouldn't say one sentence in French – was this out of embarrassment or rebellion? Nobody knew or cared. Except for her. It pained her deeply to not be able to communicate with Mama Antonia, as everyone called her. Mama Antonia was a brave soul: she fed, clothed and provided for seven children with the work of her hands. She had never gone to school and had never held a book in front of her eyes. Except for the Bible. This was the only book German missionaries have ever translated into Ewondo. Mama Antonia was a firm believer in faith, humanity and God. She never imagined her children being sent away from her to learn foreign languages and critical thinking, forgetting about their culture and the importance of the earth and water – beneath and above them.

Today, she felt confused by the expectations of her family. They wanted her to finally start living the "European dream", or whatever distorted imaginations they had of it. For her Cameroonian father this meant school, studies and a career – or better yet an *Íton* dowry, a husband and babies. She was still trying to figure out who she actually was.

She still loved to be in Y.D.E. where she couldn't openly express herself on political levels but where her spiritual self was at peace, where the streets were reddish and *sucer l'oeil* was an art form for survivors of the capital. Where girls, women and men would be sharing stories about December all year around, as well as saving money for new clothes, fresher hairstyles and innovative dating strategies. In December in Yaoundé, it rains money, so the women are extra beautiful, so the men can be extra generous. From taxi drivers to farmers, "*tout le monde est liquide*" and happy. And "Yafé" is where the fun is at. It took her a while to stop romanticizing this place, the inhabitants and their struggle. Ten years later and the culture was exactly the same – as if it had been in a time capsule. The music, the TV shows and even the stand-ups jokes hadn't really changed; it was only more of the same kind, with shinier add-ups. It baffled her how Cameroonians do not believe in *Emergence* but nobody would speak publicly about the infrastructural difficulties involved in setting up transparent businesses in a country that is used to corruption – or "*tchoko*" as it is locally known.

The memories of the past few years were still very vivid as were the current uncertainties, traveling on an identity quest from somewhere to nowhere, just away from what everybody taught her she had to be. She had had so many lives and too many identities already. She had discovered many versions of herself. Not all of them were beautiful, but a few were. She needed to remember that. On the brink of a new year, she was ready to settle, but the questions remained: where and for what? All she was certain of was the pressing urge to interact with diverse realities, to be able to recreate her own space, at her own pace.

Back in Pforzheim: the Golden City, as they like to call it, even though to her it seemed to be more of an old greyish green. Here, nobody chants or even whistles on the streets – not even on Christmas evening. Like with any other of the religious holidays throughout the year, this one needs a long preparation list. The items are diverse, from *Eierlikör* to the obligatory *Wichteln* at the workplace. Everybody is frantically waiting for an official break in their mundane lives, to finally start having fun. Because here, you have to prepare yourself, in order to rightfully enjoy yourself.

The phone rings. She realizes she was frowning her eyebrows whilst scribbling on an envelope. She looks at the time and wonders if she should pick up.

The Romantics and the Criminals

Bino Byansi Byakuleka & Sharon Dodua Otoo

> "I learned that courage was not the absence of fear, but the triumph over it. The brave man is not he who does not feel afraid, but he who conquers that fear."
>
> Nelson Mandela

He got his nickname because he was born on the first day of January. As his mother had pushed, her screams were drowned out by the cheers of the crowds dancing in the streets, hugging each other and shouting "Happy New Year!" The name printed on his *Duldung* was Richard Kirabira, but no one called him that. Even the police officers guarding the camp called him "Happy."

Most mornings at around 4am, when there was a change of shift, one of the officers would shine his or her torch into the tent and shout "Happy?!" This always confused him. Were they calling him or asking him? This morning, Happy sat outside of the tent, wrapped in two sleeping bags and was holding a cup of boiling water. Some nights before, his gloves had been stolen and he had nothing else to keep his hands warm. "Thank God for Vera..." Happy muttered to himself under his breath, as he watched her argue with the officers. She had brought a new canister of water with her when she arrived a few hours earlier. She had wanted to prepare hot drinks for those refugees who woke during the night. It wasn't enough. It was never enough.

"But it's better than nothing," Happy had assured Vera. She wiped her eyes and he put his arms around her shoulders. Ironically, he often found himself comforting her. Right now, Vera looked tired but resolute as she gestured towards the tents. She was not supposed to be there alone. It had actually been agreed at the last co-ordination meeting, that there should always be two supporters at the camp. German law required that people legally registered their protest. Of course, according to international conventions, everyone is allowed to protest, just as everyone is entitled to freedom of movement. But refugees should not get any ideas of grandeur. For in reality, it is only those who can prove their identity with some form of waterproof documentation (preferably one with a golden eagle on the green front cover) who may actually provide a signature on the required registration form. It was agreed that the protest camp was not safe for anyone throughout the night, and especially not for twenty-something female students. But – unsurprisingly as it turns out – Carl had not shown up for his shift. Yet again. Carl talked a lot during the day, but clearly could not walk much during the night. On the nights that Vera was alone, Happy stayed up too.

Happy assumed that the officers Vera was debating with were once again questioning the legality of the whole protest, as they had been doing at every given opportunity since the camp was set up two months ago. One night they had even woken everyone up and demanded to check their documents. Of course many did not have any, and slipped away while the police read the papers of the "Lampedusa" refugees. Happy had watched out of the corner of his eye, as grown men and women crawled on their hands and knees into nearby bushes. They would return later, but would never sleep deeply at the camp again. Most nights though, it was enough for the police officers to simply shine their torches into the tents to see the misery for themselves. They always called Happy. He had been identified as the leader, so he got "special" attention.

Happy watched as one group of officers climbed into a police van. There were six or seven of them. This time they were all men. Happy guessed they were about his age. He imagined how they would soon be at home. Urinating in the privacy of their own bathrooms? Crawling into bed next to their sleeping wives? Awaking to the smell of hot filter coffee and warm French croissants? The other group of officers mostly remained standing around Vera. Two policemen however walked towards Happy. He was no longer intimidated by them.

"Happy?" said the first officer. There was nothing on his uniform to identify him, so Happy made a snapshot mental note of the officer: brown hair, blue eyes, short beard, about 180cm tall, medium build. These details might be important later.

Happy didn't answer straight away, but looked the officer straight in the eye. It was a test. Which one of them would look away first? Happy won easily. The first officer cleared his throat before speaking again.

"Are you Happy?"

Happy wanted to laugh, but he managed not to. He sighed and then took a sip from his cup. In two days it would be his birthday. He wondered how the routine would go then? Amidst drunken Berliners setting off fireworks and shouting expletives at the officers? This was going to be entertaining.

The first officer looked at officer number two. Black hair, blue eyes, clean-shaven, long crooked nose, possibly has been broken before, slightly taller and heavier than officer one. Officer two clearly did not appreciate Happy's belligerence. He looked directly in Happy's eyes. This guy was going to be tougher.

"Stand up." Officer two commanded. There was a menacing tone to his voice. Happy saw two chances: simply comply and have an easy night, or play a bit, but forget about any kind of rest. It wasn't hard to choose.

"Why?" Happy answered. "I haven't done anything wrong. Why should I stand?"

But by now Vera was heading towards Happy and the two officers. Happy could not be sure that she would stay calm.

"Stand. Up." Officer two repeated. He touched his baton. This was a tiny gesture, but it sent a clear signal which immediately refreshed Happy's memory of one particularly fierce beating he had taken at a demonstration last month.

"What's going on?" Vera asked. She was breathless and agitated. She turned to officer two. "*Was wollen Sie von ihm? ICH bin die Ansprechpartnerin!*"

"It's ok, it's ok" Happy said, slowly rising to his feet. "Here you go, I'm up." He smiled cheekily at officer one and then gave officer two his best poker face expression.

"Are you the one they call Happy?" Officer two asked, looking him squarely in the eyes. Happy did not blink. He simply responded: "I am he."

Officer one shifted nervously from one foot to the next. Officer two stood firm.

"Where are the documents for the registering of this protest?" he asked.

Happy sniggered. Always the same. Always the same. He looked around at the thirty-something tents, some in better conditions than others. In the moonlight the place looked calm and peaceful. Oranienplatz had looked like this since the refugees and their supporters had arrived last October. How would it even be possible for this protest to have been going on for so long without the correct documentation? Happy would have loved at this point to have asked the officer for evidence of *his* permission to ask to see evidence of Happy's permission to protest. There was bound to be a paragraph so-so-and-so about it somewhere. Germans loved nothing more than laws and documents. Everything in this country was surely regulated by a stiff-looking East German woman sitting behind a desk surrounded by a collection of pens and rubber stamps.

"*Das hatte ich aber gerade schon mit ihren Kollegen durch!*" snapped Vera. She was cold, exhausted and frustrated. She had changed so much since the beginning of the protest. Happy didn't yet understand enough German to know exactly what she was saying, but he guessed from her tone and her body language that she was telling the officers that the paperwork had already been checked.

"*Ich rede mit dem Asylant hier...*" started Officer two. Officer one took a step back. Vera's face flushed bright red. Happy had heard that word "*Asylant*" before. Almost always from Nazis. Or people who were not too good at disguising their right-wing allegiance. Someone in one of the nearby tents coughed.

"*Er ist eine geflüchtete Person!*," she hissed. Clouds of warm air left her mouth as she spoke. Happy studied her face carefully to try and work out what was now going on.

Officer two smirked. "*Wie dem auch sei...*"

"*Hier sind die Papiere...*" Vera held up a folder. "*Nun lassen Sie ihn in Ruhe!*"

Happy held the – by now – cold cup in his left hand and reached out to Vera with his right. He pulled her to one side while the officers carefully studied the folder she had given them.

"Listen Vera," he whispered, "please, please stick to English when I am around, ok?"

She nodded. Ashamed. He had told her and the others several times that this was a refugee protest. Not a Good-German-Person-Charity-Event. The refugees were to represent themselves at all times. The supporters could translate, but could not simply take over.

"He just wanted to see the registration documents. It's just games..."

"And why did you get angry?"

Vera looked at the ground and adjusted her hair. As usual, it was tied back in a ponytail. Whenever she got nervous, she would try to make it even tighter. "He used this word: *Asylant*. It's a racist word for refugees..." She then looked back up again at Happy. "Fucking hell."

Happy watched the officers poring over the folder, trying to find something that they could complain about.

"Well at least this way, they are showing who they really are..." Vera sighed.

"Exactly!" Happy smirked "They are being honest – it's good!"

Vera felt too bitter to smile. "The way they treat you..." she muttered. "What kind of fucking country is this? Is it now wrong to fight for human rights in this–"

"No!"

Happy interrupted her with a vehemence that surprised them both. "I'm not a human rights activist. I am a human defender."

Vera looked at him slightly confused, but did not say anything because at that point Officer two approached her again.

"*Hier – eine Lücke, morgen früh um 08:00. Wer kommt dann?*" He seemed almost proud to have found something to do. Vera simply gestured towards Happy, took a step back and folded her arms. Officer two suddenly did not look quite so confident.

"Here..." he said, looking at Happy and pointing at the folder. "There is a gap. Tomorrow early. 8am..."

Happy pretended to read the folder. The officers muttered something to each other, but didn't say anything to him. After some time Happy looked up. "Puh – it's true," he said. "How did you spot that?"

Someone stirred in the tent a few metres away. It sounded almost like they had stifled a laugh. The same person who had coughed earlier? Happy guessed it was Benny.

"Just make sure that someone is here by 8am. OK?" Officer two snarled. In his opinion, Happy was altogether much too confident for a refugee living at the expense of the German taxpayer. And the refugees' collective ingratitude, symbolised by this camp, made him furious. He had wanted to shout: "You should go back to your own monkey country if you don't like our laws!" but he controlled himself. Instead he repeated: "I said, 8am. OK?!" slightly louder.

"*Jawohl*" Happy responded. It was a word he had already learned in Uganda after having watched far too many German war films. Officer two stared at him for several seconds, and concentrated hard, but could literally think of nothing more to say. He tapped Officer one on the shoulder and they both stalked off to the other officers huddled together on the opposite side of the road.

Happy checked the time: it was 4.35am. The others would be waking soon. It wasn't really possible to sleep for very long when the ground was so cold.

"Shall we make coffee?" he asked Vera. She nodded. They walked a few steps together to the protest table: the table surrounded by bags, boxes and bottles. The table which attracted tourists, food donations and homeless people during the day; and newly-arrived refugees, foxes and other, less non-racist, trouble-makers at night. One thing that police officers and activists had in common: both were there 24-7. The table was covered in wet flyers, hard biscuits, stale bread and cartons of juice. One canister was filled with water which was still hot. The other canister was broken and had sprung a leak. Happy looked under the table for the instant coffee, while Vera tried in vain to tidy the table up.

"What is a human defender?" she asked, when he stood up again. "What did you mean by that?"

"Simply this – I actually do what human rights activists pretend to do. I defend the respect and dignity of all human beings. All of them..." Happy looked across one more time at the police officers across the road, "...not just the white German ones."

Vera swallowed hard. She felt unfairly accused. Thrown into a random group of people and labelled. She wanted to defend herself and remind him that she was standing here in solidarity, and that not all white people are bad... but she bit her tongue. Happy felt the tension but was able to hold it – Vera had not experienced what he had experienced, so he could not expect her to understand. Still he was not about to make any unnecessary quick moves to make her feel better. In the past, actions like that had always taken on a dynamic of their own. Before he knew it, young white teenage girls with pierced lips and colourful hair had been advising him to end his hunger stri- ke because it was so distressing for them. Vera was better than that. And she needed to toughen up. Happy concentrated instead on spooning granules of instant coffee into each of the three flasks that Vera had gathered together. He hoped they were clean.

"Those leaders who claim to be human rights activists," Happy continued, "they don't mean it. They are the very people who make us here suffer today." He gestured out towards the protest camp. "What is his name? This your interior minister? De-Mah-zair? He is a crook! I don't want people to think I am on the same side as him."

Vera shook her head. "De Maizière doesn't care about human rights..." she said, wrinkling her brow.

"Didn't he claim he was going to stop deporting refugees back to Greece? 'Because of the terrible conditions there?' Hypocrite! On the international stage he will fight for refugees. But at home when no-one is looking he kicks them in the teeth..." Happy was talking himself into a rage. He willed himself to calm down.

"But human rights activists are not all like him..." Vera started. She was be- ginning to feel defensive again.

"No, not all," Happy agreed. "No, some come here and try to tell us how to run our protest and force us to eat vegan food..."

Vera smiled. Happy once told her he was shocked that people in Germany treated their dogs better than their children. She couldn't really argue with him.

"...that's why I call myself a 'defender.' I defend and I leave the human rights talk to the romantics and the criminals."

"Are you calling me a romantic?!" Vera's eyes narrowed into a slant. But at that exact moment she dropped the sugar. The crack of the tin on the pavement woke some of the people in the tent closest to them. Benny, Happy's best friend, was anyway a light sleeper and had been coughing for hours before he fell asleep earlier. Happy and Vera could hear the others shifting and turning in their sleeping bags while Benny coughed and spluttered his way out of the tent. He staggered towards Happy and Vera, stiff from having lain in an awkward position on an unforgiving floor in sub-zero temperatures. Benny was sick, but did not want to take anyone's advice to move to the nearby unused school building, where mothers with their children, the elderly and the disabled had long since moved.

"You will have to carry me there then!" he would joke, before coughing again. Sometimes it was so bad, it sounded like his journey on earth would end right then and there. This morning, once the coughing had subsided, Benny patted Happy on his back and asked:

"Why?"

Benny was one clear head taller than Happy and twice as wide. He could have sent Happy flying with the pat on the back. Benny took care, but Happy still flinched.

"Why what?" Happy responded, rubbing his back.

"Why all the noise?" Benny clapped and rubbed his upper arms. He had two coats on, but neither of them fitted him well and the zip on the outer one was broken.

"Hey, it wasn't me!" Happy proclaimed, "Vera was trying to throw things at the police again – I tried to tell her..."

For the first time that evening Vera laughed. It was a quiet, shy one, but a laugh just the same. "I'm going to get more hot water" she smiled, before picking up the only functional canister and heading off in the direction of the nearest late night corner shop. "I'll be right back."

"Wait!" Benny said, turning towards her. "I want to apologise for my friend." He gave Happy a side-eye.

"Ahhh! Benny just leave it!" Happy snapped. "Why are you getting involved?" He knew what was coming. Benny always defended the supporters. He deferred too much.

"You guys sort it out..." Vera said. She then looked Happy straight in the eye. "I know why I'm here." Happy looked straight back. Vera really had changed. He looked at her with new-found respect. Then he nodded. And he meant it. Vera turned and walked away.

Happy handed Benny a cup of coffee, knowing what Benny would have wanted to say if Vera had stayed. Benny could also be romantic at times. But maybe this was not a bad thing.

"What about the police?" whispered Benny, once Vera was out of earshot. "There are no citizens here..." Benny was deeply traumatised by his whole experience with the German police since he had been in this country. He had been regularly stopped, searched and brutalised for the slightest offences. And even such treatment that was a walk in the park compared to the strategies practised by the Nigerian officers in Abuja. Benny shook, and it was not only because it was cold.

"Don't worry," Happy responded, looking at the police officers sitting in their vans, engines running so that their heater would stay on. "We are good for at least another 30 minutes. It's too cold for them out here."

Benny sniggered. "Even for the Germans, it is too cold here?"

Happy nodded. "Yes, even for the Germans..."

Boom

Clementine Burnley

Mimi knelt to pour brandy into the small metal beakers that doubled as tooth mugs. The heat of the day seared through her clothes and suffused her nerve endings with tension that was beginning to ground itself in contact with Anke, like tiny bursts of static. The couple had been sailing along the rocky stretch of Red Sea coast all day. The cove had looked inviting enough for a quick evening swim, after a day spent knotting strands of net together on the hot deck of the *Hilda Wenger*. Mimi had packed a picnic for afterwards, the red and white blanket she reserved for crossing borders and a cheap tourist map on which she outlined the countries they left behind. This time she would draw a line around Eritrea. The women would cross into Djibouti waters the next day. The trip was a last attempt to rescue a relationship that was going as cold as the Munich winter they had left behind.

Equally dark-haired, Mimi and Anke were at first glance similar enough to be mistaken for siblings. Anke had been compared to JFK, her height balancing a solid frame that complemented Mimi's pre-Onassis Jackie. She brought a quality of intense attentiveness to their relationship that Mimi quickly realized was impersonal, habitual to all her interactions. Anke's focus lasted until she had drawn a conclusion after which, curiosity satisfied, she would say: "Light-headed", or "religious" and move on to someone else.

Mimi had never known Anke to change her mind about one of these labels, once she had decided on it. Anke would spend time with the person, on a day trip, or over a lengthy meal and then announce her findings. There were no grey areas. Determined to escape Anke's judgment, Mimi learned to invent and present new aspects of herself to her partner, and to make this task look effortless. It was this deceptive certainty that had drawn Mimi to Anke in the first place. They had met in Berlin and moved in together after three months of furtive meetings in the cinemas around Kreuzberg. Anke had been interning with a patent law firm in Mitte. Mimi had given up both of her lovers and the cooperative where she ran integration courses for foreigners. When Anke had taken over her father's legal practice in Munich Mimi had moved with her. In the five years that followed she had created a life that perfectly complemented Anke's professional activities. To compensate, Mimi's natural competitiveness emerged in a compulsive ordering. At her parties, she was known for politely but relentlessly probing her dinner guests, until she had their biographical details and had sorted them into a social hierarchy.

As Mimi waited on the blanket with lukewarm alcohol, Anke was reluctantly retracing her steps to where the *Hilda Wenger*'s dinghy was pulled up away from the waterline. Mimi had left the mosquito repellent on the first aid box, along with a large part of their picnic; crackers, hard dried sausage and tinned olives. When Anke looked back at the water, the narrow craft was emerging from the shadows around the island. Mimi shuffled, planting herself firmly between shifting stones and shading her eyes, peered out onto the random glitter of sunlight on water. Until then, they had shared the sandy cove with only the translucent lizards that clung to the rocks above their heads. The Red Sea adventure they were on, had crystallised in Mimi's mind after five days of icy Munich rain. Anke had opened a letter from a former colleague who was working with the German Foreign Services for a year in Senegal. She read it out loud to Mimi as they sat by the window staring at an iron-grey sky.

"Abene is a tiny village with no electricity, or running water… My German language students are an inspiration, so bright and enquiring. The day begins in the ocean, work ends at sunset… I am learning to play the Djembe."

Mimi had heard only a series of disconnected phrases, thinking in between about how Anke was beginning to exhaust her ability to recreate new selves for her consumption.

Perhaps a change of scenery would make Mimi more interesting. When they met Mimi had been living with two women in a squat in Neukölln, teaching German to Kurdish doctors and nurses as part of the process of getting their qualifications recognized. Mimi had tired of the intense emotions and the shared bathroom. Anke had seemed exotic in her orderly stolidity.

Mimi had watched Anke replace the letter in its creased envelope, a distracted look on her face, and had spent the rest of that week on a holiday exchange website. The house in Cairns, Australia, looked idyllic, verandahs overlooking a waterhole, cane furniture, a rainbow striped hammock. Anke's response had been definite, but disappointing.

"In real life we have no plans to ever go to Australia."

She had brooded for a few days, then made contact with a woman who lived in a treehouse in Ontario.

"Too cold. Not in winter."

Anke's counter proposal as a post-script to fairly pedestrian sex had astonished her in its boldness. The Bab el Mandeb straits combined danger with exoti-cism. Mimi read out loud to Anke, an infomercial for adventure diving tours:

"The straits were originally a land bridge between Africa and Asia. Thousands of people were supposed to have drowned when a prehistoric earthquake ripped the two continents apart..."

Mimi was at once pleased and annoyed at the morbid romanticism of the language and the way it entirely avoided mentioning the slave trade and the more recent wars in the region. The hundreds of sunken wrecks that sheltered tropical fish might have been placed there especially for the tourists. Over dinner in their retro-chic Munich apartment, their friends had seemed gratifyingly stunned to hear Anke had agreed to leave a lucrative patent law practice for months in a part of the world they had trouble finding on a map.

So far, the trip was not making Mimi exciting to her partner in the way she had expected. What she did not realize was that her partner was miserable too, but had accepted the way she felt as an inevitable part of being human. Anke simply took other people's happiness as a lack of depth. Mimi's dilemma was, that most of the time she found neither Anke nor herself deep and that, seemed unfair.

After their video recorder escaped Mimi's inexpert knots early on in the trip and crashed into the salon wall along with the small television, they had been left with well-thumbed playing cards and a dwindling reserve of conversation. Mimi had developed an elaborate series of rituals to ward off tedium interrupted by bouts of intense fear when she would lie awake, feeling Anke's chest rise and fall with her breathing. Anke slept annoyingly well; often she fell unconscious mid-sentence. While waiting to fall asleep herself Mimi would look at Anke's mouth as it hung slack, the skin starting to bag loosely under her chin. In the morning Anke would awaken, refreshed and unaware of Mimi's spying.

Mimi excelled at scuba diving, one of the few sports, which her athletic partner did not. Anke would join her occasionally but mostly Mimi escaped into the sea alone, persisting even after her ears had begun to ring constantly and Anke's voice acquired an echoing quality that lasted for days at a time. Today's dive had been unusually eventful. A lazy hunt had led her across patches of sand, where dark fronds of algae undulated with the quiet passage of eels. Growing bored, she had followed a school of fish. The bright figures had slipped through gardens of coral and vanished into a hulking shadow. The grey green surfaces of the dhow were coated with a mixture of liquid muck overgrown in spots by a solemn sculpturing of barnacles and coral. The curved spine rested on pebbled sand. A few strokes away the continental shelf fell into cold darkness.

The enclosed space inside had been crammed with indistinguishable objects; fishing nets, a wheelbarrow. She had felt a slow dragging at her insides, propelling herself forward to where scores of deathly still figures had settled haphazardly into the lower end of the tilted hold. One of the bodies was clearly female. In the curved gap between the dead woman's legs a cluster of tiny bones had settled into the silhouette of an infant. Mimi had startled, thrashing for a short moment at a gentle touch to her ankle and turned her head.

The diver blinked at Mimi, whose eyes bulged, shocked. Unlike Mimi, this woman swam without a mask or diving bottle, relying on the single breath in her lungs. Graceful hands extended before her, tilting gently at the wrists a few times and then clenching into fists, thumbs up, accompanied by a slow nod as she kicked out long, slim legs, propelling herself away from Mimi. As the distance widened between the two, Mimi calmed, swinging her legs out in front of her to hang motionless and stare at the young diver, eyes beginning to burn. The woman gestured at the sloping deck, her face constricted with emotion Mimi had trouble deciphering. A couple lay wrapped together in a skeletal embrace, the skull bones impassive, dully reflective. Breaking for the surface, Mimi ripped off her mask and looked around her to see the woman half a dozen yards away, and closing the distance between them quickly. Mimi had introduced herself in a mixture of halting English and rapid fire German, gesturing with a fine-boned hand towards the yacht to make clear that she was not alone. The diver was called Leyla.

"I thought your boat was drifting out of control."

After watching the water for some time and not seeing anyone come to the surface Leyla had decided to start a search and had found Mimi in the hold of the dhow.

Together, Leyla and Mimi proceeded to explore the wreck more thoroughly, finding more bodies in the main hold.

Leyla had tired first, the up and down effort to breathe shortening the time she could spend underwater. In the end the water had turned yellow with tiny sea creatures and they had both given up, unable to see. Clinging to the ladder of the *Hilda Wenger* Leyla had struggled to formulate jumbled feelings in German at Mimi's asking if they should get in touch with the local Coast Guard. Leyla disagreed:

"They have travelled far enough already, why separate them now? They look peaceful as they are!"

Mimi stared, uncomprehending and it took several tries before she nodded, finally convinced. Before swimming back to the yacht she had taken Leyla's hand, holding it in hers for a short while and releasing it with a firm nod. She had been waiting all day to find out what Anke thought she should do next. Without mentioning of course the guilty tenderness of the underwater graveyard. Leyla was difficult to fit into her partner's definite world. There were no in-betweens, no grey areas for Anke. Still Mimi planned to tell her this evening after the two had watched the sun go down together.

When Anke returned from the dinghy, an older man was following, gesturing and talking rapidly all the while. The difference in height between the two, forced the stranger to hold his head at an awkward angle, looking up at Anke as they walked toward Mimi. She watched them approach from where she sat on the scratchy blanket, and thought distractedly that she had only packed two glasses. The old man was slight of build, and looked pleasant, his open face seamed with deep groves carved into leathery, olive skin. Mimi looked back over the water. It was sunset and wind-scavenged dust had turned the sky into a pastiche of pinkish and orange, mixed with yellow gold. They were going to miss it. She had been looking forward all day to evening, the picture-postcard view and the tumbler in her hand. Mimi sighed, shoulders dipping, and turned towards the ill-matched pair.

Anke looked helpless at the stream of conversation coming from the old man. She motioned towards Mimi for rescue. Her limited stock of Amharic and intuition had apparently run out on the walk back. Anke said:

"Do you have anything for him?"

The old man called, urgently this time and beat with his hands against the air, ignoring the beaker Mimi held out.

"We don't want to buy anything,"

Mimi said this in English, repeating the phrase several times in German when the old man appeared not to understand. With each repetition she raised her voice further. He shushed her, looking at the ground where Mimi was standing. He seemed frightened.

The birds had been streaming over the water since dawn, single-minded in escape from the damp and cold of a northern winter. Now the ospreys called down to the trio on the beach as they scattered in all directions from the rising wind. Mimi and Anke looked up, distracted, as both had been at intervals all day by the feathered conversations above their yacht. The old man had listened, settling into stillness while she spoke and then took her hand firmly; he was strangely cautious in his movements as he pulled Mimi away from the neat square of striped cloth she had laid out on the sand.

"Boom, Boom!" He was whispering, panicked.

"Anke, please!" Mimi's tone was more irritated than alarmed, but the muscles of her face were tense, matching worry lines between her eyebrows, eyes puppy-desperate above full lips that would usually curve into a pleasant smile but were now pulled tight and turned downwards. As Anke took a few uncertain steps, the old man pulled Mimi toward the water. He was surprisingly strong, teeth showing white under a neatly trimmed moustache. The words fell out of his mouth in a liquid rush, too fast for her to pick out meaning. Except for the whispered sound he made over and over again "Boom, Boom!" Shoving him suddenly away, Mimi had broken into a run, screaming in her headlong dash back towards Anke. She remembered too late that some parts of this coast were seeded with unexploded mines from the war. These Russian-supplied devices were triggered by sound and rapid vibrations.

A lone fish hawk was scudding across the water ready to strike when a cataclysm of metal lifted the sand, sending red and white striped fragments of cloth fluttering high. Startled, the bird pulled away steeply through a fine layer of white grit, which drifted down through the screaming air. The explosion scattered the contents of the basket far enough for the old man to find two green passports and a thick wad of currency intact in a waterproof envelope. Later on that evening he would finger the creased notes thoughtfully before handing the money to the soldiers who turned up to secure the area. The passports he would tuck away in the inside pocket of his shirt.

Support a Black-Owned Business Especially at Christmas

Njideka Stephanie Iroh

Snow in a city seems unnecessary. It looks enchanting for a while, as the first flakes settle and enwrap streets and rooftops in glistening white. The hectic pace of the city slows down. But soon, snow gets mucky and slushy. It becomes a nuisance; dogs pee on it, cars drive on it, roads get icy. Emergency rooms are packed with patients with broken legs and arms from minor accidents on slippery pavements and zebra crossings. Delays on public transport due to heavy snowfall mean you can never know whether you will be delayed by only five minutes or so late that you are better off staying at home entirely. No-one ever knows when the next train, tram, or bus will arrive and I have often found myself cursing when the No. 13 drives past me one minute after I have chosen to embark on the 20 minute journey on foot after having waited in vain for 30 minutes. You can't ski in the city, not that I would ski anyway. In fact, I dislike skiing, snowboarding and ice-skating, any type of winter sport, really. As far as I know, the lyrics were "walking in a winter wonderland" and not "slipping and sliding in a choleric white Christmas village."

The weeks counting down to Christmas are not something I look forward to. In fact, I don't look forward to Christmas at all. I have nothing against the actual celebration or festive season. After all I could choose to avoid that if I wanted to. It's the pre-Christmas fuss, the so-called "traditional celebrations" and the mood of the city during this frosty and hectic period, which alienate me. The upside is that shops are open longer on weekends; the downside is that shops are open longer on weekends. Department stores packed with endless queues of grumpy Viennese customers buying gifts for their partners, children, friends, bosses, enemies or neighbours – all so they can wrap them and send best wishes from the *Christkind*, the Christ Child, a little white angel that brings gifts on Christmas Eve.

Christmas markets, decorated with bright yellow lights and Christmas ornaments, serve as outdoor pubs during the Advent period. You can find stalls there with all sorts of different hand-crafted accessories, chocolate-covered fruit, and alcohol. These markets are the winter spots for family outings at the weekend, and after-work punch and *Glühwein* during the week. This scalding winter beverage with wine as its main ingredient and an assortment of different fruits (depending on your fancy and what the vendor of your choice has to offer) is a bitter-sweet experience of bliss and blisters. The scent of warm wine, cinnamon and orange peel lingers in the air and a person immediately knows that there is a Christmas market nearby with slightly less grumpy and possibly drunken Viennese customers.

I can't help but wonder what all this has to do with me. Like my two closest friends Iya and Akanya, I try to avoid these Christmas in the city scenarios. I have run out of excuses to give my colleagues during the Advent season when they ask me to join them for *Glühwein* after work. Mostly because I have found myself lured into awkward drinking sessions in the cold with people who have the urge to share their unwanted opinions with me. Alcohol tends to encourage random acts of stupidity as we know and I have found I am never quite drunk enough at Christmas markets or parties to deal with the idiocy that awaits me. On one occasion I was invited for a round of punch, in the course of which I genuinely wanted to punch someone. I accepted the invitation, which was very unlike me because I'm a loner. At the office I engage in as little conversation as possible. I was waiting for my second cup of *Glühwein* at one of the packed stalls when my colleague Gerald pulled me aside. He was wearing a ridiculous Santa Claus hat that last saw a washing machine three winters ago. The bobble on the top was no longer white, but a revolting yellowish-grey. I imagined that his cat must've got its claws on it, chewed it and possibly peed on it; probably because she was also fed up of seeing him wear the same Santa hat year after year. Gerald was very annoying, most likely even to his own cat. His cheeks were red and his wandering eyes were blood-shot and glazed. I didn't want him to touch me so I quickly followed him, showing him he had got my attention. He had pulled me aside to make conversation with me and I wondered why. He cleared his throat and asked me if I wanted another drink. "I just got a refill," I said. Gerald smiled, his eyes not able to focus on my face and he asked me what turned out to be on my top five list of random questions at the most inappropriate of times: "What do you think about police brutality against Black people? Is that a thing? Does that really happen?" I stared at the bobble on his filthy Santa hat and said nothing, but thinking to myself, "Merry Christmas and bottoms up!"

In situations with colleagues like Gerald, or even random people in day-to-day life, on the bus or at the supermarket, Tupac often comes to my mind because all eyes are on me and it's me against the world. We're talking great rap but it's not a great way to feel. I don't want to go through every day with these emotions, so I reach out.

Last winter my friends Iya and Akanya organised a Kwanzaa festival workshop with me. All three of us follow our daily work routines consisting of nine to fives, studies and part-time hustles but whenever we have the chance we make time for the labour that is close to our hearts, lifts our spirits and helps build our community. By celebrating Kwanzaa we wanted to take an African

Diasporan approach to a season in which white Christmas not only meant white snow and white angels but also white children in blackface, supposedly representing the Three Wise Men.

During the month of December we met up twice a week to prepare the programme. Iya was in charge. Iya was *always* in charge. She is a mother in the way she loves and a best friend when it comes to confiding in her, or having a night out with the girls. She has the life experience, the care, and love for her people without the judgement. She never gives me the feeling that I know less than her because she is older and wiser, but instead shares her perspective. But Iya doesn't take any nonsense from anyone. She often tells me I am too soft when people stare at us on the tram or make racist remarks and I ignore them. She flicks her locks when she gets in her real talk zone and she will simply be honest, voice stern, yet eyes kind. Though she may complain about it a lot, she loves her Village. That's the thing about Vienna: It simply has a hold on some people.

Akanya smiles a lot. She's a practical thinker who dreams big, but always keeps in mind what is doable. She stays focused and lovingly reminds us of our work when Iya and I wander off into our creative exchange and forget that there are deadlines to be met. Akanya often talks about leaving the Village and living somewhere else. She seems to be looking for a better place to live. She had moved away to France some years ago, but came back for reasons she did not share. Her two daughters were little at the time and hadn't yet started school. She came back two years later just in time for her girls to start primary school. They no longer speak French fluently, which Akanya still regrets. She had made the move for her children. She had an aunt in France whom her daughters adored. Aunty would speak to them in Igbo and French and take them to African markets to buy beautiful materials and their favourite ingredients for Sunday lunch. But the Village was calling and to Akanya's aunt's surprise and disappointment her three girls had left France.

I wondered why some of my friends came back after having moved away from here. I wondered but I wasn't even ready to try. I stayed put, not leaving but living with that slight desire to be gone, with my feet glued to the heavy pavement and with *Fernweh* in my belly. Akanya wears hers on her sleeve; she hasn't swallowed it or attempted to hide it. Her *Fernweh* is written in her smile and coats her words. She always makes the best of her current situation and brings joy to many people. She would be missed should she move away again.

We always made time to go for lunch after our meetings. After our last session before the Kwanzaa gathering, we wanted to treat ourselves to something special. "We need to celebrate," Iya said, tying up her locks into a bun, putting on her woollen hat and tugging it into place. "Where should we go?"

"Do you fancy Italian? There's a place up the road where they do a nice risotto," I suggested.

"Well, that's basically rice, isn't it? I'm not sure I'll like the way it's prepared. I'm picky about food, but you know how much I like rice!" Iya said.

"How could I forget?" I teased. "It's serious business: You and your Jollof rice, fried rice, plain rice. Should I go on?" Iya laughed and shook her head. "I'm too hungry for this conversation."

Akanya made a suggestion that pleased us all: "Let's go to an African restaurant. I think it would be nice to support a Black-owned business. It fits the spirit of Kwanzaa. Do you remember that delicious catering we had a few weeks ago for the children's festival? I think that was Ethiopian. Let's do that."

We set off to the tram station. It started snowing heavily and the thick snowflakes landed on my lashes and stuck to my coat and scarf, irritating me. I didn't want to talk on the way. I would have just complained about the weather. Once we arrived at the tram stop, the frustrated herd of people waiting there made it obvious that there hadn't been a tram in a while. The loudspeaker announcement that followed with a crackling noise was barely audible and confirmed my assumption that the snowfall had caused delays on the No. 5. Iya said what I was thinking: "You'd think it was their first winter with snow! Why wouldn't they be prepared for this?" I thought how ironic it was that we complained about Vienna quite a bit, and had also internalised the art of moaning in such a perfectly Viennese manner – well, almost. I shuffled my feet back and forth hoping to warm them up but trying not to splash too much snow and slush on myself or others.

The tram arrived shortly afterwards with fogged up windows. Children had drawn Father Christmas with their fingers on the window – next to profane words. There were far too many people packed into the tram for any of us to have a comfortable journey, but we were determined to squeeze ourselves on because we were hungry and had no idea when the next tram would arrive.

We arrived at a restaurant decorated with little Ethiopian flags and statues. There was no music playing, which was a relief because I knew that if I heard another Christmas pop song I might not have managed to swallow my food. There was only one customer in the two-floor restaurant, a white Austrian woman at a table set for one person. She was just finishing her meal as the waiter approached her with a smile and asked, "Is everything to your satisfaction?" The woman gave the waiter a fake smile and said that it wasn't quite what she had expected or was used to. He nodded, smiled, replied with a quick "OK" and said that he would soon return with the bill.

When the waiter, a short, middle-aged Ethiopian man, approached us he wasn't smiling. He didn't seem happy to be receiving any more customers. He was running the restaurant on his own that day. We sat down in a cosy corner and he brought us two menus. "Do you have rice?" Iya asked before the waiter could ask us anything. I couldn't quite believe how Iya was being about her African food choices and I had to laugh thinking that she probably wanted Jollof rice and plantain. "Rice?" the waiter replied in a tone that suggested Iya was not serious. "Rice? This is an Ethiopian restaurant! If you want rice, you can go to a Chinese restaurant. We serve injera." "Yes, I know," Iya said bluntly, "and I don't like it." I pulled my lower lip sideways and bit it gently, waiting for the waiter's reaction. I was already nervous. He looked stern, but replied calmly: "I can make you rice, white rice, but it will take forty-five minutes."

"Forty-five minutes? FORTY-FIVE minutes? What? AH-AH! Why? Do you have to ship the rice over? Has it not gone through customs yet? Why would it take almost an hour to serve rice?" Iya was on a roll and could have kept going because she was hungry and very impatient, but the waiter interrupted her: "Look, it's up to you. You decide and make your order. Tell me what you want to eat and I will make it. In the meantime let me take your drink order." We ordered our drinks and Akanya and I chose vegetarian dishes. I knew Iya didn't intend to be rude, but the communication with the equally impatient waiter made me feel uneasy during what seemed like an endless discussion about rice. I picked my dish quickly and with little attention and eagerness.

Iya was on the fence about ordering the forty-five-minute rice, but she was very clear about the injera. She didn't like it. She said it in the tone five-year-olds would use to speak about their least favourite food, so Akanya encouraged her to order the rice. Akanya then kindly offered to go find the waiter, as he seemed to have forgotten about his three hungry customers.

Akanya was determined for us to have a delicious meal. As she got up she told us that she wanted our experience in a community restaurant to be a peaceful and joyful one. "We need that," she said. I followed her, curious to see how she would talk to the neglectful waiter. I leaned on the bar next to the kitchen listening and watching as Akanya swung her head round the corner and looked in. But she didn't get very far with her words. The waiter was sitting at a small table in the kitchen with his friend. They were eating. He turned to Akanya with his mouth full and took a large gulp before shouting, "Can't you see that I am eating? I'll get back to you when I am done!" Akanya froze. She looked at the waiter, with her arms folded, leaning against the door frame of the kitchen. She stood slanted, cool and calm. "My friend has decided to have the chicken dish but with rice, so I would like to order now." The waiter seemed irritated. He waved Akanya off and got up from the table where his friend was left eating slowly and seemingly pleased with his lunch.

When Akanya and I returned to the table she told us that she was having second thoughts about having lunch at this restaurant. I too, was disappointed. Going to this restaurant wasn't just about having a decent meal. Being here was also about enjoying our food and each other's company in a community space. It was about the expectations we had when we entered an African restaurant and imagined stepping out of everyday experiences and alienation. To me supporting a Black-owned business meant creating more spaces of freedom.

The waiter returned shortly after Akanya's complaint and, to our surprise, had prepared the two vegetarian dishes. Iya told us to start while the meal was still warm. I was relieved that the food looked delicious. After all the waiting and tension and rice, not rice, I simply wanted to eat. I broke a piece of injera off, dipped it into the lentil sauce and popped it into my mouth. It was cold. I turned to Akanya who began chewing in slow motion and shaking her head. Iya motioned to the waiter to return. "The food is cold," Akanya said.

"That's not possible. My friend and I just ate from the same pot." The waiter folded his arms and hissed at us as he spoke. He didn't look any of us in the eye.

Akanya made a point of looking the waiter straight in the face as she spoke to him. "Well, this food is cold. Both of our plates are cold and we will not eat cold food."

The waiter raised his voice as he yanked the plates from under our noses: "Fine then! If that is what you claim, then I will warm the food." I remembered how the waiter had treated the white customer earlier. It could have been a coincidence. Maybe we were just unlucky, but it made me feel very uncomfortable that he was snapping at us and was polite to his previous customer. I was upset and wanted to leave.

"Do you know what?" Iya said, as if she had read my mind. "That won't be necessary. I'd like to cancel my order. We no longer want to eat at your restaurant. You have been nothing but rude from the moment we walked through that door. The fact that you chose to let us wait here while you were eating your lunch, your tone... This is really not how we want to be treated in an African restaurant. Honestly, this is no way to do business either. We are going."

The waiter had started walking towards the kitchen and turned around to face us, gesturing towards the door with one plate in each hand. "Then leave! Please leave! I do not want you here. Go. No, wait, wait, wait! You did not pay for your drinks!" Akanya had already started putting on her coat and Iya wasn't wasting any time either. I didn't want to leave without paying for the drinks, not with the way the waiter was screaming. "Let's just pay for our drinks," I suggested to the girls, but they insisted we leave. "It's about principle. We can't let him treat us like this. We are customers, we pay for service and that was not it," said Iya.

I felt like a teenager under peer pressure as I put my coat on and moved towards the door. "I'll call the police!" the waiter shouted.

"Oh, call the police then, do it. We don't care. We're leaving." Iya wasn't worried at all as she yelled back at the waiter. She was convinced that we were in the right.

We left the restaurant and buttoned up our coats as we walked. We didn't know where we were going; we just wanted to finally eat lunch. The road the restaurant was on was long and busy. The snow had stopped and it was much colder. I didn't know whether we were walking briskly to warm up or to get as far away from the restaurant as fast as we could. We didn't walk fast enough. The waiter was following us. I heard his voice and turned around to see him frantically making a phone call: "*Polizei? Polizei! Ja, kommen Sie.*"

At first I thought he was pretending to call the police to frighten us. He followed us and didn't slow down. By now I was feeling very uncomfortable. I asked Akanya why we couldn't just pay for our drinks to avoid the embarrassment and stress of dealing with the police, but she kept walking and told me that everything would be okay. Yeah, right.

Traffic was slow with careful drivers minding icy spots on the road and pedestrians sliding across the zebra crossing in the slush, but the police car was the slowest vehicle on the road. It had to be because the police were looking for us amongst the passers-by. The police car pulled up and I stopped walking and wished I could disappear in a hole in the ground. This was the first time anyone had called the police on me. Living in Vienna as a Black person you often hear people threaten to call the police for no particular reason, but I had never been in the situation of dealing with them after such a threat and here was a Black man doing this: my embarrassment turned into pain and ultimately anger. Was it really necessary?

Two white police officers emerged from the car. Iya, Akanya and I waited as they approached and I noticed the waiter's friend from the kitchen was also making his way to the "police intervention scene." This was getting even more absurd. The policeman who took charge was older than his colleague.

He started asking questions, while the younger policeman stood and watched. He appeared to be inexperienced and slightly lost. He folded his arms tightly across his chest, stood straight and looked strict, but still seemed as though he had only just graduated from the police academy. I thought of what this young white man in uniform embodied for us, at such a young age. And then I thought of my colleague Gerald and his stupid hat.

The Viennese dialect is a sluggish form of German. It sounds like some words are being drawn apart very slowly and yet stick together the way chewing gum would. The words embrace the air and linger, even when they are offensive. The language of the Viennese serves as a very creative way of discussing, cursing, and insulting. Often things don't seem quite as bad as they are when you hear words spoken in this dialect, especially because of the so called Wiener *Schmäh*, which is specifically Viennese humour. These particular Viennese policemen did NOT speak to us in High German.

The policeman asked the waiter what the problem was, as protocol required. He gave the impression that he certainly had more important and interesting things to do than to intervene in this case during his afternoon shift. He sighed heavily as he leaned forward to get exactly what the waiter was saying.

"These women did not pay for their drinks," the waiter said. "They are thieves! They came into my restaurant and wanted to make trouble, then they left without even paying."

The policeman turned to us and asked whether this was true. "Well," Akanya said, "he was extremely rude to us, so we saw no point in paying for his service. We refuse to pay for cold food and bad treatment."

"What do you mean cold food? My friend here also had the food, tell the police, my friend. Was it cold?"

"No, no! It was not cold. The food in this restaurant is de-li-cious. It is exquisite! You will not find food like this in any other restaurant…"

"OK, alright, get to the point," the policeman said, interrupting the waiter's friend and newly-found witness.

"…and anyway, I think that they planned this because they don't have any money!"

"Yes," the waiter agreed, "they don't have any money, they cannot pay!"

"What? No money? What?" Iya was furious. She grabbed my wallet which I had ready in my hand because all I had wanted to do was pay and get out of this awful experience. She took some twenty and ten Euro notes and waved them in the waiter's face: "What's this then, eh? What's this? What do you call this? Your behaviour is disgraceful! You have disgraced us. I will tell all my friends and no-one I know will ever eat at your restaurant again!"

The policeman interrupted Iya and told us to pay for the drinks and forget everything that had happened. We were about to pay when the waiter shouted: "No, that is not enough!"

The policeman took a deep, slow breath through his nose with his eyes shut and said: "*Wos wuinzn bitte noch? Sui i sie festnehman? Jetzt beruhigen's Ihna amoi*", meaning: "What do you want? Would you like me to lock them up? Calm down." But the English translation doesn't quite capture the true meaning of the words coated in Viennese sarcasm and flair.

We gave the waiter the money and he took it, but he was still not satisfied, because we had not been "punished."

"Right, then this has all been sorted out and we can all be on our way," the policeman said.

Iya was still very angry and had plenty to mutter to the waiter, as the policemen started walking towards their car. The younger policeman who had been quiet the entire time turned to Iya and told her to calm down. He gave her a glare that made me feel anxious, but Iya, being who she is, confronted the policeman: "What are you lookin' at?"

Akanya and I stood on either side of Iya and pulled her with us. "Let's go sis. Let's just go and forget all of this." The policemen, clearly irritated, got into their car and drove off. We turned away from the waiter and his friend who made their way back to the restaurant down the road. As we walked, linking arms with Iya in the middle, we couldn't quite believe what had just happened. We shook our heads and half laughed, chuckling in disbelief and shock. We walked and I forgot how cold it was.

Akanya wanted us to enjoy each other's company and what was left of the afternoon. She let go of Iya's arm and started running and sliding across the ice. She ran a few steps and let her feet glide along the patches of ice, testing how far she could go. She was smiling and I had to smile too. She looked beautiful and happy and I wondered if maybe winter and snow weren't all that bad after all, not if I had my sisters with me.

Once we had walked a considerable distance, Akanya reminded us that we hadn't managed to have lunch. We laughed and agreed to walk into the next restaurant we could find. We came across a Chinese restaurant further down on the same road. We sat down at a table in a cosy corner and before the waiter could utter a word, Iya impatiently interrupted him and asked: "Do you have rice?"

Very Christmassy

Tigist Helen Schmidt

Ben kisses her on the lips.

His lips feel firm and dry. There is a light wind lifting the humid Los Angeles air away from Sarah's bare shoulders.

"This dress… wheee!" he laughs, "and of course I go crazy for red and green dresses at Christmas!"

He extends his hands, stretching his arms out like Frankenstein and staggers around her in a half-circle so he can hug her from behind.

She bats him away: "My hair Ben! How many times, not the hair!"

It's up in a chignon that has taken her three tries and twenty hairpins.

He looks contrite but Sarah knows he doesn't really get why he can't run his fingers across her scalp every time he's nervous. Once, when she was walking past a pet store she had wondered if he needed something warm-blooded he could groom. One of her summer jobs had been to take well-trained family dogs into retirement homes and to make conversation while the dog and old person bonded. The old person was always calmer at the end of the visit. The expression on Ben's face reminds her of the old person's before the stroking begins.

Ben touches Sarah apologetically on the arm then rings the doorbell. No one answers and after a few more, frustrated short pushes on the concentric brass nub, he fumbles in the pocket of his crumpled blue jeans. "I hope I took it with me…." he mumbles, still looking. "Granny turns her hearing aid off and plays Beethoven on full blast to make Mom crazy." And then he turns to Sarah: "I hope you brought earplugs." Ben's eyes roll about in his head. He is trying so hard. Sarah giggles and at long last feels at ease. She takes a deep breath. Finally success: he pulls out a single key, which he dangles in triumph in front of her nose. Sarah is indeed starting to feel Christmassy.

She had been really disappointed earlier on in her apartment when in response to her softly voiced: "Babe?" silence had followed. So Sarah had repeated herself, annoyed: "BABE!" She had waited and then suddenly heard the sound roar out of her mouth: "BABE!!! What do you think of this dress?"

Ben had looked almost scared of her. He put down the empty beer glass he'd been taking to the kitchen. The bottom had made a cracking sound on the side table.

"It looks great babe. Very "CHRISTMASSY"."

Sarah had been suddenly, perhaps unreasonably annoyed and confused. "Nettled" her mother called it. She thought it perfectly described her nervous prickliness at the thought of meeting his folks. But instead of telling him why she felt this way, she stared at him coldly: "What does THAT mean?"

Ben shrugged: "I don't know. It's just very... red and green."

Sarah had been frantic all afternoon, trying on different dresses, shoes and accessories in front of the mirror in her bedroom. There was a huge pile of different clothes on her bed, the floor and the chair. And she still had nothing to wear. Ben had listened to her pacing back and forth for most of day and had run out of patience with her frantic freaking-out monologue.

"...want to be festive, but then I also want to be conservative..."

"...need to take a shower. I am sweating again..."

"...This was just not a good idea. Maybe I should tell them that I am sick. But I already did that once before... Maybe I should have a drink...?"

Ugh!

Sarah had looked at her phone to check the time. Another deep breath and a good look in the mirror. Fleeing the mess in the bedroom for the toilet in the hallway, she forgot to close the door properly and had to get up and slam it shut before he heard the ladylike plipping and plopping. *Too much realness will kill the romance!* These were her mother's words, not hers. They were first said across a dining table in Addis Ababa. It's funny how her mother's voice had followed her across borders, all the way from Ethiopia to Dortmund and now LA. At some point she had internalized her mother, like an unwelcome buzzing, some tinnitus of the mind. The thought was not comfortable.

"I don't know. I should have just celebrated Christmas with my own family in Germany."

Stomping into the living room, where he was braced, ready for another brisk flurry of accusation and counter-accusation, his crumpled white T-shirt and jeans made him boy-like and fragile. She had thrown him a dirty look instead to disguise the rush of love and vulnerability, which had come over her. There was a basketball game on TV. He had motioned apologetically at his ears, and taken another sip of his beer, hoping that she would not ask him about her dress. As he drinks, Ben allows himself to remember the scene in her bathroom earlier that morning. Four outfits before, Sarah was shimmering in golden sequins and looking in the mirror. Ben had watched her from the bathroom door. She looked amazing but he knew he couldn't say that yet again.

"You will be fine." He said tentatively.

Only for Sarah to respond as she had twice already that day:

"I am black and German. Your grandmother *double* hates me!"

Ben smirked involuntarily. It was a nervous tic that drove her mad:

"She is like a hundred years old, man. What is she going to do?"

Sarah's face had scrunched up in distress at his stock excuse. He still didn't get it. Sarah had experienced too many times how people interpreted her blackness as a threat. It was a sad fact that in the United States being black could even get you killed. For Sarah, anytime she met new people: anything was possible.

Ben could still not believe the thought of meeting his completely colorless JA (Jewish, American) parents would make her so unreasonably afraid. He was not in the habit of thinking about his grandmother when he could avoid it. She was the Kryptonite in his anti-racist family.

So instead Ben had smiled and hugged her.

"What if she says some shit?" Sarah had whispered. But he obviously didn't hear her. He just gave her another kiss, this time on the cheek, with more smiles.

Ben began to feel a bit nervous. Perhaps he should have prepped his grand-mother on his girlfriend's Ethiopian and German heritage. Giving up on a response, Sarah went back into the bedroom to snatch up her jacket and purse. Ben watched as she walked back in, her steps jerky and short in the formal heels. She stood for a moment in front of the TV and then switched it off with the words:

"We got to go."

It had taken the length of the car ride for Sarah to explain how she was feeling, with Ben nodding, after checking his mirrors, and occasionally letting go of the steering wheel to pat her hand while he looked at her soothingly. The drive to Ben's grandmother's house seemed endless. When she let him kiss her outside the front door to his childhood home he felt both triumph and relief.

Ben opens the unlocked door and allows Sarah to go in first. What happens next is hard to explain. Later on, she will describe the scene to many different people. She will not always be believed. What Sarah sees, is a tiny old lady running toward her, pausing to snatch up a red baseball bat that is somehow leaning on the wall beside a wooden chair in the hallway. Her thoughts come disconnectedly as the old lady picks up speed on the stripy hallway carpet. She is quite close to Sarah now. Sarah is still more surprised than scared. Does Ben play baseball? Sarah cannot remember Ben ever mentioning baseball bats but from what she sees on TV every red-blooded American male has one. Even so, what is it doing at the entrance? Or has the old lady been told there will be an Ethiopian for Christmas? The tiny lady starts swinging the bat at Sarah. She is shorter than Sarah, and so directs the angle of her swing upwards. Ben's grandma looks…absurd. One hysterical giggle escapes Sarah as she tries to work out if she is more shocked by the cartoon-style violence or by the words this white-haired small person is snarling as she continues to lunge and swing.

"Who the fuck you think you are? Coming in..."

The bat is very close this time and so Sarah steps hastily backwards to avoid being hit, loses her footing and falls on the floor. She squirms, close to tears as she wonders what Ben is thinking of his bright idea now: an Ethiopian celebrating Christmas with secular Jews. Ben is beyond embarrassment. Avoiding Sarah's accusing eyes, he focuses on getting his grandmother to behave like the sweet old lady who has received past girlfriends' with polite conversation and, after some months with genuine warmth. The humiliation escapes into his voice as he tries to calm his grandmother down: "Granny! GRANNY! GRANNY!

The shouting brings an older man, rushing from the dining room to see what is going on. He adds to the noise: "Mother! Mother!"

Sarah is still on the floor watching Ben and presumably his father, Joshua shout and struggle with Ben's grandma. Joshua must be more used to dealing with his mother than Ben because he manages, after a short but decisive tussle, to get a hold of the bat and shamefaced, he puts it back in the hallway. "Mom, this is Sarah, Ben's girlfriend. Remember, I told you about her?" he says awkwardly.

Granny looks at him skeptically. While she says nothing at all, it seems obvious she thinks he is lying to her. Clearly, Joshua hadn't told his mother what she really needed to know about Sarah. Still, the old lady examines Sarah from head to toe as she lies, limbs sprawled, dress crumpled, on the floor. Sarah moves to her knees, getting up on her own, still in shock but recovered enough to be pissed off that Ben does not think to offer to help her off the floor or dust her off. But she can see that Ben is doing his clumsy best to lighten things up: "Granny, most people start with the introductions and move on to baseball after lunch. This is Sarah. That's my girlfriend!"

Granny looks, unsmiling, at Sarah's curly hair. Then looks at Ben. Then looks at Joshua: "Hello Ben. Hello Sarah."

Granny stomps off to the kitchen before Sarah can say anything back. Joshua and Ben seem off-balance again but politely, they ignore their discomfort in favor of compliments: "You look great in that dress, Sarah!" Joshua says and nods at Ben enthusiastically and taking the cue, Ben whispers to her, puppy-dog eyes hopeful: "It can only get better from here."

"Well, really..." she thinks, smiling her thanks at Joshua, who grins back at her, "...how could it possibly get worse?"

Joshua finally seems to have run out of optimism and small talk, but Ben manages to produce a stiff smile every time Sarah looks at him. All three sit on the couch and stare silently at the lit candles on the Menorah until a woman who must be Ben's mother, wanders in with a tray of what she loudly announces are "Kosher biscuits!"

It is getting stranger and stranger. Sarah looks for a hearing aid to account for the volume of her voice, but she is not wearing one. The woman is about sixty. She seems not too steady on her feet, the biscuits sliding off the tray as Ben and Sarah jump up simultaneously to greet her. She looks a bit out of it: "Hello dahlin'! How are you?"

Sarah is looking enquiringly at Ben as she responds: "I am well, thank you. How are you?" She does so although Ben's "Hey mom" means this must be Lilly.

Sarah is beginning to feel sorry for Ben. Perhaps this is why he yells in his sleep and on waking, clings to her body like an anchor. Which is partly why he has been sleeping on the couch lately. It's unfair anyway because Ben could have warned her but then she would probably not have come with him to this bizarre household.

Lilly has been in the bathroom and has missed the entire scene at the door. It takes a while to explain to her the "misunderstanding" in the hallway, which is what Joshua and Ben are calling it. A misunderstanding. Lilly watches them try not to stare at her nostrils, which are lightly dusted with white powder and giving up the story, begins to wave the tray of biscuits again, interrupting the men with: "Biscuits anyone?"

Ben and Sarah at the same time say "No, thank you." while Joshua reaches for one and bites into it: "Yum. Did you make this?"

Lilly shakes her head and points to the kitchen: "Granny did." She watches them all glance at her nose, places the tray next to the Menorah, brushes her face clean with the tips of her fingers, and sits next to Joshua on the couch. They sit in a row, not saying anything to each other. Ben is squeezing Sarah's hand as she scans the room, which is heavily decorated with black and white family pictures of Eastern Europe and Jewish ornaments. There are no posters of famous baseball players. Lilly can't sit still – she nervously plays with her hair with one hand and finds new ways to rearrange her skirt with the other. Unconsciously copying his son, Joshua tries to take Lilly's hand, but she will not let him. Joshua breaks the uncomfortable silence, getting up with: "I am going to check on Granny." All three nod as he disappears, only to leap up in unison as he screams from the kitchen: "Mother...Mother...Mother... Mother!"

Lilly has trouble getting her feet to move in a straight line but then she follows Joshua's voice, trying not to trip. They meet Granny face-down at the table next to the Shepherd's pie. She is not moving an inch. Joshua tries to wake Granny up by shaking her, but she is terribly still. There is a repeat of frantic activity that erupts when the front door opens and again Sarah has trouble understanding what is happening. Everyone is doing something fast and loud. Ben is calling 9-11. Lilly is panicking and going back and forth. Sarah is watching the scene unfold like a TV show. Granny's eyes are open and fixed to the ceiling, mouth wide-open. Sarah hears herself murmur:

"I've killed her. OMG. OMG. OMG. If it wasn't for me she would have not freaked out and reached for the baseball bat. I killed her on Christmas. On Christmas! OMG. OMG. OMG. This is the worst Christmas ever. What am I going to do? Ben and his family will hate me forever."

The ambulance arrives and the paramedics rush down the hallway pushing a gurney, the baseball bat flying, as they push the wooden chair out of their way and pound into the kitchen. They lift Granny onto the gurney. She lies pale and still. Her eyes are closed but her face is turned accusingly towards Sarah.

Everything else seems to happen in slow motion. Lilly and Joshua rush out with the nurses. Ben throws Sarah the keys to the car. It seems he is expecting her to follow them to the hospital because he actually calls out: "Babe, follow us!" over his shoulder.

Sarah is frozen with the guilt.

She watches them leave.

The keys fall to the floor.

Whtnacig Pnait (Watching Paint)

Sharon Dodua Otoo

BAM!!! The front door slammed shut as I bolted down the stairs from our seventh floor flat – DOOSH! DOOSH!! DOOSH!!! – stomping past Samsa on the fifth – MiAOW! – and skidding 'round the yak on the third – iiiiiiH-HHH! – needles everywhere when I reached the first. The junkies were back. I wasn't running 'cause I was late, I was ESCAPING. I just had to get out of there.

BOOM!!! The main door bounced off the concrete wall in the hallway as I threw it open. I've been told a million times not to do that. Coming soon: one million and one.

As soon as I reached the street corner my shame, hurt and frustration erupted. I swore at the top of my voice while throwing my school bag in one direction and my glasses in the other. I heard them KRRRAX! on the pavement. Lots of people rushed by on the way to somewhere or on the way back from so-mewhere else. Some really were in a hurry. I could tell because they had that "don't-mess-with-me-boy!" look on their faces – their eyes dark and harassed, their shoulders hunched up to their ears, trying and failing to defend their necks against the biting wind. But some were only pretending. Those were the hipsters, just moved in from New York or Stuttgart or Prenzlauer Berg. They looked shifty and embarrassed as they jogged past. Probably because they didn't have proper jobs to go to. All of them ignored me. All except Mustafa – who anyway wasn't going anywhere. I knew that he would be watching me from over the road, slurping his coffee and flicking his cigarette stub to the ground. I breathed heavily through clenched teeth, tight fists and tears. Most mornings are pretty bad. This wasn't even my worst.

Don't give up.

Moments passed, as did two blue-eyed toddlers being cycled to Kindergarten in an expensive-looking trailer. They gaped at me from under their hand-knitted woolly hats. Their gaze was met by my middle-finger.

"Eh! Was soll das...?"

Turkish accent. Instinctively I looked in Mustafa's general direction – but I could only see blurs of various colours and sizes, so I carried on turning my head, trying to style it like I had actually planned to turn away from him all along. I was still furious, but at least I had stopped sobbing. From the corner of my eye I could just make out the blobs, which were probably Mustafa finishing his coffee and throwing the empty paper cup into the gutter. He crossed the street, walked up to my school bag and then squatted over it.

"Leave it!" I snarled.

But of course he ignored me. Instead, he started to pick up everything that had fallen out of my pencil case – well everything that could still be saved. He also found three of my abandoned school books and caught most of the various loose sheets of paper that were dancing annoyingly around my feet. I had long ago stopped trying to hide how bad my writing is from everyone, but I still didn't want Mustafa picking up my things.

"*Lass das!*" I repeated, this time in German. I did that because I still could not speak this stupid language fluently yet, but I wanted to surprise him into leaving my stuff alone. He ignored that too and just continued to work in silence. I wiped my eyes. Although I wasn't crying anymore, the wind was icily cold and it froze the tear-tracks on my cheeks. Everyone I knew who had visited Germany had warned me about Berlin winters before I moved here – but nothing had prepared me for this. It was only November and I was already forced to wear ugly long johns underneath my jeans. I was wearing two jumpers, my mum's ski socks and a thick scarf I found in lost property last week – but I was still in danger of losing my fingers to frostbite. I looked around for my glasses and found them literally seconds before some random dog ran up and peed on the spot where they had been. Mustafa took the glasses from me and handed me back my school bag. Sulking, I reluctantly hung it over my shoulder. It was a bit wet because my drink bottle had not survived my tantrum, but apart from that everything else was fine. Damn him.

I stole a glance at Mustafa as he quietly worked on my glasses. He had unzipped his jacket and rolled up his jumper to reach the T-shirt underneath. He cleaned my glasses on the once white fabric, breathing on both lenses every now and then as he did so. After that, he bent the arms gently back into place. The left lens was cracked but for some reason it was still secure in the frame. He nudged me when he had completed his work and wordlessly signalled to me to put them back on. I did, and then I looked across the road, focusing on the small market there. I could just about make out Mustafa's dad as he continued to stack the carrots on his fruit and veg stall. We didn't have much to say to each other, Mustafa's dad and me. My Turkish didn't stretch further than "*Günaydın!*" He didn't speak English at all (Mustafa said he refused on principle) and his German was even worse than mine. So whenever I visited them at home, Mustafa's dad and me – we mostly just smiled at each other a lot.

"*Bitte schön...*" Mustafa grinned, wrapping his scarf more tightly around his neck. I knew that was a hint, but even if I had been planning to say "*Danke*" I definitely wasn't going to now. Idiot. For a second, I thought about saying that all out loud – but it definitely would have ended painfully for me and it wouldn't have been worth it.

"Go to school," Mustafa said, after a few minutes of competitive silence.

"You go!" I shot back, squinting at him menacingly.

Mustafa sighed and muttered "*Verdammte Hacke, Junge...*" under his breath. I had no idea what it meant. He knows how much I hate school, and I hate it even more when he says things I don't understand. But I didn't want to ask him what he'd just said. I didn't want to talk to him at all. I just stared back down at my feet and wiggled my loose tooth with the tip of my tongue. And I kept my mouth firmly shut. Even in the few minutes we had been standing outside, the temperature had dropped again. It was so cold, my teeth had begun to hurt. Though my nose, lips and ears were getting numb, I could still feel enough to tell that Mustafa was looking down on me, his eyes heavy with disappointment and responsibility. He brushed my Afro gently. I looked up to ask what he wanted, but in that moment, Mustafa spotted one of his friends across the road and gave him a silent nod. The friend nodded back, then came over to us. I gave Mustafa's friend a smile, hoping it was weak enough for him not to feel encouraged to talk to me, and focused on my tooth again. Mustafa leant over to him, and gestured to me.

"Siggi, this is Anokye –"

Ok, it's true that it was difficult to hear, because in that exact moment a bus driver blew her horn angrily while driving past. Another one of those bike riders with a death wish had crossed her way. But "Anokye" is only three syllables. It isn't THAT difficult to say. And Siggi isn't exactly a name that you come across every day either.

"Woah! What a strange name! Anok-? Ano-what?" Siggi said demonstratively. Even though he looked straight at me, I don't know if he was speaking to me. It sounded like he was starting a comedy routine for everyone near enough to listen. "Ano-chair?" he continued, "Where does it come from?"

Mustafa nudged me.

"Timbuktu," I lied. I always said that in moments like these. I don't even know where Timbuktu is.

"Ahh...Africa, right?!" Siggi's eyes began to glimmer romantically. I think the word "Safari" also left his mouth. I could see that he was excited about something, but I had already mentally switched him to mute. I looked at Mustafa – he rolled his eyes and shook his head apologetically. I looked back at Siggi – his lips were still moving. I remembered that back in Hackney, there was a kid who looked a lot like Siggi. They had the same kind of wannabe-Black uniform: baggy trousers, Air Nikes, and a big gold chain. The Hackney kid's hair was slightly longer though and the freckles across his face made him look way too gullible to be gangsta. Anyway, I once punched Hackney kid in the face so hard that I bust his lip and cut my knuckles on his teeth. Drops of our blood stained the pavement and formed a curious pattern: like a red ink-blot picture of the Golden Stool. Hackney kid cried when I refused to apologise. His parents threatened my parents, but I stood my ground. It's one thing to make fun of me because I am still reading comics while everyone else in the class is reading classical novels. I can swallow that. But when people start to mess with my name – then it's all over. Siggi was damn lucky that Mustafa was here to protect him.

After Siggi had gone, Mustafa lit another cigarette. He watched me as he smoked. I couldn't work out the expression on his face. He seemed to be sizing me up. Making some calculations. Looking back, I guess he was working out if I was ready. Eventually he flicked the cigarette away and clapped his hands together. I squinted at him: now what?

"Stay here..." he commanded. He crossed the road, zipping his jacket back up and pulling his hat tighter over his head to cover his ears. His straight hair struck out from under the hat like bolts of jet-black lightning. I saw him talk briefly with his dad, who at one point looked over at me and nodded, before giving Mustafa an apple and patting him on his back. They both laughed. I looked away. Too late. The sight of them laughing played non-stop in my mind, like one of those animated gifs. I clenched my fists again.

Don't give up.

Mustafa crossed the street one final time that morning, eating the apple as he approached me.

"Let's go" he said, before taking another bite.

"Where?" I said. "To school? Forget it..."

"Let's go!" Mustafa interrupted me.

And that was that. I had not wanted to go, but I didn't really have anything else to do. And even if Mustafa didn't care about me, at least he was bloody good at pretending that he did. Since moving to Berlin, Mustafa was just about the only person I saw outside of school. Apart from my mum.

As we waited on the platform at Kottbusser Tor my mood finally got better. Mustafa stared straight ahead and whistled. He was calm and that helped me to feel the same. I was already standing quite close to Mustafa, but I leaned a little closer and hoped he wouldn't notice. I closed my eyes and breathed in: a mixture of cigarette smoke, coffee, sweat and cheap after-shave filled my nostrils. I stifled a cough. No wonder this guy was still single.

"*Eh! Was machst du?*" I opened my eyes and looked up. Mustafa looked slightly disgusted and pushed me away. "*Hau ab!*"

I took a couple of steps back and said nothing. Luckily, in that moment the train arrived. He watched me warily and made sure that I got on first. There were enough free seats for us to be able to sit down next to each other: the first miracle of the morning. Normally the U8 is "standing room only" at seven fifty. I fixed my gaze on the view through the dirty, scratched-up window. My vision was no longer distracted by the tiny images of the Brandenburg gate tattooed all over it.

As the train left the station, Mustafa asked: "Why you don't like school?" I simply carried on looking at the various shades of black that whizzed before my eyes. I could see absolutely nothing and that's about how much I felt like saying, in answer to such a stupid question.

"*Junge, Schule ist wichtig*", Mustafa added. I knew he knew I didn't understand so I just carried on ignoring him.

"I didn't finish school," he continued "You did know that before?"

Actually I didn't. I didn't care either. I looked at Mustafa and raised an eyebrow. It could have meant "so?" or "really?" depending on how generous Mustafa's interpretation was.

"Or did you think I dreamt all my life of being a carrot seller?" Mustafa laughed. His laugh turned into a lengthy smoker's cough. But at least the questions had stopped. For now. I sighed and rolled my eyes as I thought about the 20-minute journey ahead of me. And about how long Frau Dernburg would most likely shout at me for being late when I did finally reach school. And then how much she would shout at me again, a few minutes later, for not having done my homework. And then again, maybe an hour later, for not having made any notes throughout her lesson. I thought about how I would probably once again spend the entire lunch break sitting outside Herr Fischer's office: watching them, watching me. How I would receive another letter to take home to my mum. Of course the evening ahead of me would mostly be taken up by her shouting at me for my "terrible behaviour this morning", for breaking my new glasses, for me losing my drink bottle and for me bringing home yet another red card from school. No one ever said anything good about me. There was nothing good to say. My life was a collection of disastrous moments knotted together by a desperately thin string of hope that there was some point to it and that I would understand it soon.

Don't give up.

I spoke after Mustafa had finished coughing.

"I would rather be a carrot seller than a school kid, Mustafa. Trust me." I looked at him straight in the eye. "School is so boring...it's like watching paint dry. It's killing me."

Mustafa sighed, but didn't say anything. The train pulled in at the next station – screeching in fact, because the brakes needed oiling. All the passengers winced, except Mustafa and me. Moritzplatz. I knew it was Moritzplatz because the recorded voice announced it. And because I have travelled this line now so often, I would recognise it even if I was listening to music and couldn't hear the voice at all. Or even if I was listening to music and had my eyes closed, I would be able to feel where we were by counting the number of times the train had stopped. What I definitely would not be able to do would be to read the station's name. And that wasn't because of my cracked lens. Not the newest glasses, not even a telescope could help me, because the letters in the words I read just don't stay still.

Moritzplatz.

Could also easily be Mtroizpaltz or Mrtiozpatlz or Mitorzpltaz.

It makes no difference to me at all.

I wiggled my loose tooth with the tip of my tongue again. The doors to the train opened and there was a kind of collective struggle as impatient people tried to get in, although several even more impatient people were still trying to get out. Mustafa sniggered just after someone made a comment, which was probably a really awesome diss. I really need to learn to speak this damn language. And then that robotic beeping noise signalled that the doors were about to close again.

"Ok, get ready," Mustafa whispered. His voice was dark and mysterious and, although he had not been threatening at all, I felt the need to run again. As the doors banged shut and the red light above them stopped flashing, I began to panic. Mustafa grinned secretively, just like he had looked when he had said goodbye to his dad a few minutes ago. He knew me well enough by now to know that, even if it killed me, I would not ask him what was going on.

Now something was different about the train, the way it moved away from the platform. It seemed to hover above the tracks. I heard and felt nothing except that weird feeling you sometimes get when a plane is taking off. Only two or three other people looked around the carriage with a confused expression on their faces. I wish I could have gone and stood next to them. I would have felt a little safer. I tried to ignore the way Mustafa was smiling at me.

And then, just like that, the people around me started to clap rhythmically. I didn't hear the music until a few seconds later. Most were bopping their heads and rocking in their seats at the same time. Some of those who were already standing shifted slightly from foot to foot. Everyone else leapt up and started to dance. Really. Rocking hips and elbow jerks. It was as if everyone in the train had been under siege until the moment the doors had closed and they were now all celebrating the end of a war. When I next looked at Mustafa for some kind of clue, he just winked at me and continued to grin, before turning his attention back to a woman sitting across the aisle from us. I could tell by the way they were looking at each other that I was going to have to find someone else to talk to. By now, the lights had dimmed and I could hear the music in the background. It sounded like something out of a Bollywood film. Only the mirror balls were missing.

The train was still gliding effortlessly through the darkness. It was one of those really long ones without carriages, so whenever there was a slight turn I could see quite far down – almost all the way to the other end. I'd never thought about it before, but it was full of yellow poles and handrails. Normally passengers held onto these, knowing that if they didn't, one swift move could make them have even more unwanted body contact with another passenger than necessary. That rarely went down well. But here, during this smooth journey, no-one needed yellow. Everyone I looked at was talking and laughing – some people were even hugging each other. I could just about make out two girls, towards the front end of the train, dancing in the middle of the aisle. The girl on the left wore an ankle-length dress. It was light blue – I think they call it Royal Blue in England – and decorated with sequins and glitter. Her long black hair was tied up in a ponytail, which swayed back and forth as she turned her head in time to the music. A piece of cloth was attached to her hair, the same colour as her dress, and this flowed down her back until it disappeared into the general flow of fabric and rhythm. Her dancing partner looked like her identical twin, except she was dressed in pink and silver. Their hand and hip movements matched exactly. I was fascinated. The last time I had seen this kind of dancing was at an Indian wedding in Bethnal Green. I didn't think something like this was possible in Berlin. Not even Kreuzberg.

"Diwali."

I turned to my left. The voice belonged to an older woman who was sitting right next to me. She was one of the few who were not on their feet. Because she was holding onto a walking stick, I assumed she was not able to dance. Her greyish hair was tied quite closely together in a small bun. It surprised me that she wasn't wearing a hat like almost everyone else. She also had a red Bindi on her forehead.

"Pardon?" I stammered.

She leant closer to me and whispered. "Festival of light. Diwali – it's a Hindu fes..."

"I know what it is," I interrupted. I was a bit embarrassed that she was explaining it to me, like I was an outsider. She smiled and relaxed again back in her seat. But now I felt awkward because actually I had a million and one questions I would have liked to ask her. I thought about saying sorry, but in that moment the crowd cheered. I turned back to my right to see the girls dancing again. They were getting closer to where we sat. In the meantime, Mustafa had moved across to sit next to the woman he had made contact with. They did not speak at all. They just looked deeply into each other's eyes and held hands. It was a bit disgusting to be honest.

"My name is Sita," came the voice from my left again. I was relieved that she wasn't angry with me after all. When I turned back to look at her again she offered me something that looked like fudge. I normally don't take anything from people I don't know. But I thought my mum would not mind if I made an exception this one time.

"I'm Anokye," I responded, smiling and taking the fudge.

"I think you are from London too?" answered Sita.

"How can you tell?"

"I heard you when you were talking to your friend. Your accent. I think somewhere north of the river, right?"

For a short while I could only nod and chew. I was surprised myself about how emotional this moment was for me. I think in my whole life no one had ever before guessed correctly where I come from, after I told them my name.

"I used to live in Stratford," Sita continued. "Have you worked out what's going on yet?"

Of course I hadn't. And it was so surreal I decided I would not tell anyone who wasn't here that it had happened at all. They would never believe me. I took a deep breath and thought back again to that gif-moment where Mustafa and his dad had laughed.

"I know it has something to do with Mustafa," I answered. "At least, I know he knows something about it."

Sita nodded. "This is his UBOC," she replied. "He catches it every now and again when he needs to... how shall I say this?" She looked at Mustafa and smiled. I looked at him too and then quickly looked away. They were kissing?! What the?!

"Well... we all need to stock up on positive energy every now and then, don't we?" she finished. I noticed her hands trembling slightly as she handled the fudge. This reminded me of my dad's hands. I tried to brush that thought away.

"UBOC?" I asked tentatively.

"Sorry... it stands for *U-Bahn* of Colour."

Although Sita spoke with an unmistakable London accent, it was when she said "colour" that I thought I heard a slight tinge of an Indian one too. I wanted to ask her about that, but the dancing girls reached Sita and me in that moment. The three of them spoke to each other briefly in a gentle, lulling language that I didn't understand. It definitely wasn't German. At one point they all laughed and somehow managed to include me in on the joke, although I hadn't got it at all. The girl in pink touched my arm and a warm feeling surged through me, starting from her palm and spreading instantly to all parts of my body. It felt a little bit like warm creamy hot chocolate was flowing to the tips of my toes, to my fingernails, to the edges of my earlobes. It was the first time I had felt warm from the inside in Germany. I liked it a lot.

"They know you..." Sita smiled at me as the girls had danced away... "One of them lives in the same block of flats."

And instantly my mind went back to the junkies and the needles and the vomit on the floor.

"I hate that place," I said. "I really hate my mum for making us move there – I thought Hackney was bad..."

"Yes, I used to do my grocery shopping on murder mile."

And with that, I remembered that Hackney had not been all that great either. But at least I knew my way around there. I had had my friends, my uncle and my auntie. There was fish and chips, baked beans and prawn cocktail crisps. There was "*Only Fools and Horses*," "*Eastenders*" and Cartoon Network. People were polite there. Even the racists were well-meaning and friendly. And I could speak my language – not this weird English that I had to force my tongue around, so that I had any chance of being understood. Sita looked at me for a little while, waiting patiently for me to carry on.

"We came because my dad died. He had Parkinson's Disease."

"I'm really sorry. When was that?"

"About a year ago..." I bit my lip. I was nervous about where the conversation might turn to. People sometimes react very strangely when I tell them my dad is dead. "My mum was offered a job here..." I finally continued, "...and Berlin is very cheap she says."

"It is," nodded Sita, offering me another piece of fudge. "I think your dad would be proud if he knew how much you are going through, and yet still surviving."

I smiled whenever I imagined that my dad might be watching me from somewhere. I often wondered if he could read my thoughts. "I think he is already back on earth," I said after a few moments. "That's why I called my cat Samsa. I think my dad is actually hanging around here in Berlin with me..."

"You read Kafka?" Sita sounded very surprised. I didn't blame her. Why on earth would a twelve-year old boy know anything about '*The Metamorphosis*?"

"My mum read the beginning to me." The girls had reached the other end of the train now and were dancing back towards us. It was still loud all around us, but somehow this wasn't a problem. Sita and I could still hear each other.

"I did a project about Kafka in school. It took me so long to finish it. Mum stayed up three nights in a row, she typed everything that I said."

"Did you get a good mark?"

I shook my head. "My teacher laughed and told me that I had just cut and pasted it from Wikipedia."

"What?!"

"In front of the whole class..."

Sita was speechless and I didn't know what else to say. The girls had reached us again by now. As they twirled and swayed, the music began to get quieter.

"Heinrich-Heine-Strasse!" the recorded voice announced. In response the crowd clapped louder and faster. Some of the younger people stamped their feet. The dancing girls bowed in appreciation before laughing, hugging and then finally clapping for each other. They moved back through the carriage, waving and hugging as they went.

"I love Mustafa's UBOC" Sita smiled. "There is always one celebration or another. I always make sure to catch it." She handed me yet another piece of fudge.

"This is delicious," I said munching, glad that we were no longer talking about school anymore.

"It's Barfi. I made it myself."

"Oh wow. Could you teach my mum how to make it?"

Sita laughed. Her eyes shone when she did so. "Even better, I can teach you how to make it!"

As the train approached Heinrich-Heine-Strasse everyone began to settle down again. The dancing girls, who had already reached the other end of the train, were now putting their coats back on.

"Listen," Sita said, taking a piece of paper and pen out of her bag. "I am getting out here." She scribbled something down. My stomach turned. "Get in touch with me, ok?" she handed me the piece of paper.

"I... I can't read" I mumbled. I was ashamed to admit it, but I wanted to be friends with Sita and if I couldn't contact her, I might lose her forever. She stood up slowly and limped towards the door.

"This, you can" she smiled. "Get in touch with me, ok?"

I nodded. She stepped out and she was gone. Mustafa returned to his seat just by mine. White people began to enter the train and the mood returned to its usual grey blandness. Newspapers went up and smartphones came out. We travelled on to the next station in silence. I clutched Sita's note in my hands and stared out of the window. I felt strange and alone. Mustafa's UBOC had been fun – but it had been his place to stock up on positive energy, not mine. We arrived at, and left, Jannowitzbrücke and I barely even noticed.

"What's that?" he asked me, pointing to the note, as the train began to move again.

I gave it to him. I would have liked my privacy. I would have liked to protect Sita from Mustafa's rough energy. I braced myself for a stupid joke about me having fallen in love with an older woman. But I did want to see her again. I had no choice.

"What is this?" he asked, giving it back to me.

I looked at it myself for the first time. Then I smiled. Then I laughed out loud.

"Daer Aoykne,

Lte's meet aiagn – vrey soon!

Pelsae cmoe viist me.

I wlil sohw you how to mkae Bfari.

Dno't gvie up!

Mrs. Sita Patel"

She had also added her phone number. I read the note several times over and over again...

Alexanderplatz. Then some unintelligible information in German. Then some more unintelligible information in English.

Don't give up.

Don't Give Up.

Raw

Monique Simpson

'Fuck. Him. And those shitty little minion friends of his can fuck right off, too. *Arschloch*! I HATE you!!! How could you – how dare you…? Why did you…? And then you… Arrrrrggggggghhhhh! *So ein Scheiss*… Shit…'

This was the internal conversation that Rachel had in her head in repeat, over and over again until it embedded into her brain like a ravenous *Ohrwurm*, but the song that was stuck in her head was far from cheerful; these melodies expressed relentless anguish and hate and grief.

Rachel's mind raced through every word that he had ever said to her that she had held dear. '*Ich liebe dich*… I love you… I want to be with you forever… I'll never leave you… Let's name our child Abigail…' She had held these words very closely to her heart. Replaying all of these moments in her mind, listening to the words, and reading his body language; every syllable felt like she was being stabbed, repeatedly. Yet she clung to those words like an addict.

Rachel's mind had stopped when he said as he was dumping her, "Maybe sometime in the future, we can be together." She had analysed the way he stared apologetically, yet seemingly sincerely into hers. Tears had begun to form in his hazel eyes. Rachel had heard the tone of his deep voice rise to a higher pitch and begun to break. She had watched in slow motion as he uncomfortably shifted his body weight from side-to-side. He had kept on combing his curly hair back with his fingers, as he did every time when he was nervous.

"Maybe sometime in the future, we could be together," she said, mockingly. 'Oh yeah? Well maybe you can kiss my arse, you little prick – how dare you? Who the hell do you think you are?!' Rachel let out a sinister cackle.

'…And you believed him, you idiot!' She laughed even louder and then began to cry inconsolably. Tears flooded down her full cheeks and into her palms. Rachel's face and her head hurt her.

These feelings erupted from inside Rachel like a volcano at the sight of Tobias parading his new girlfriend with tanned skin and long brown hair at Kurt's New Year's Eve party. She froze when she first saw them. Tobias' head slowly turned in her direction until they locked eyes for what seemed to be an eternity. She died for what felt like forever, but he just continued to greet the party guests. The way that they effortlessly worked their way around the room, his joyous facial expressions, her sickening giggle, and how everyone just seemed to just fall at their feet, all triggered a whole host of emotions that were too much for her to handle in a room packed with ecstatic revellers. Rachel quietly left the party and aimlessly roamed the streets of Vienna. It was freezing, but Rachel did not feel the cold, because her blood was boiling. She stopped here and there to use an object to prop herself up during one of her crying fits, like a door, a lamppost or a step, but she just kept on walking while her eyes remained fixed ahead replaying the events in her mind.

Reds and whites – all she could see were blurs of reds and whites, interspersed with greens and yellows and pinks and blues. The smell of smoke was still quite strong despite the fact that the fireworks proudly proclaimed the beginning of the New Year a while ago. The Christmas decorations impressively flashed and shone brightly along Vienna's dark streets. In a single moment of clarity she could make out one massive, sparkling red ball hovering above her, while neon lights enticingly beckoned her with their repetitive swirl-shaped movements. As she walked along the street she saw that exquisite crystal chandeliers were elegantly suspended over her. She realised that she was on Rotenturmstraße and smiled weakly as she took in the sights around her. 'Schön...'

Then she remembered that this was the very street where Tobias first told her that he loved her. They had gotten into an argument, for the umpteenth time, about the stares that they received when they affectionately walked down the street together. Rachel was oblivious to the stares; it was just something that she never focused on and she somehow managed to block it out. However Tobias noticed every single time it happened. He felt like he was being scrutinised and it made him feel deeply uncomfortable, so much so that he would sometimes react in an aggressive manner towards the gawker. She would tell him to calm down; he would try to justify his actions; she would tell him in a roundabout way that he was being too sensitive and that he should just forget about it, and then the cycle continued. But on this occasion on this particular street, he had said, "Let's give them something to look at." So he put their shopping bags down on the floor, he grabbed her hands, and he began to slowly waltz with her in the middle of the street, while he hummed a tune. And as they moved around to the count of three he whispered in her ears that he loved her and that he didn't care what people thought.

This memory caused her to inhale sharply and then she began to choke. She struggled to breathe, not from the haze of smoke around her, but because her pain was suffocating her. Rachel reached out and grabbed hold of a lamppost to steady herself as she tried to calm down.

"Whyyyyyyyyy?" was the only word that could come out of her mouth, between her cries and her gasps for breath.

'Inhale… Exhale… Inhale… Exhale,' she repeated to herself. She could see her breath in front of her, and the puff of white cloud gradually began to form and disappear more slowly to a consistent rhythm.

'Get up, Rachel, now – get. Up!' As she said that, she mustered up all the strength she had to pull herself up; she felt heavy and weak. All she knew was that she had to keep going, she just had to get as far away from him, as possible – somewhere, anywhere, just as long as he was not there.

She sped past the imposingly broody gothic structure of St. Stephen's Cathedral and kept on going. She broke into a jog, which turned into a run as she picked up her speed. She turned left here, and she turned right there and she kept on in this fashion, running, until she came across a wide road. The odd car went by, taking the owners to their various destinations after the night's celebrations.

A car horn sounded, "Beep, beep, beeeeeeep,". "*Glückliches neues Jahr,*" shouted one jovial passenger to Rachel as it sped past.

However, Rachel didn't hear any sound; she didn't even blink. She was locked in concentration, stuck in time. She was scrutinizing his face in front of her; trying desperately to see if he was suffering as well; searching for any tell-tale signs that he had changed his mind and desperately wanted her back, too.

She loved this part of Vienna, it was so romantic with its picturesque streets and impressively yet now eerily lit grandiose buildings, because of the haze of smoke that surrounded them; the white Greek-styled Austrian Parliament Building with its large columns and its impressive façade; the monumental gothic-styled town hall; the Rathaus with its tall tower. Yet Rachel took no notice, instead she meandered through the streets of central Vienna, a blubbering mess, with muffled cries of pain. Eventually she stopped abruptly and vomited.

'Well this is flipping ironic,' thought Rachel as she wiped the spit from her mouth with the back of her hand. Panting heavily, she adapted her eyes to her surroundings. Eventually, Rachel noticed a series of large residential buildings and staggered towards a tall greyish building with row after row of windows. Pfeilgasse. She sat on a wall opposite the building to rest for a bit. She used to live in this building as a student. In fact it was here, during at a corridor-warming party on the sixth floor, where she had first met Tobias. She remembered the heated debate she had been having like it was yesterday…

"No, you can't be from England," a man had said, speaking in an Austrian-heavy accent. "Where are you from?" He was wearing round, frameless glasses that were slightly bent out of shape. He had on a light blue and white-checkered shirt with short sleeves and black trousers. His hair was styled in a faux hawk, in an attempt to conceal his receding hairline.

"Well I was born and bred in England, as they say, so I am from England..." Rachel had smiled, but she was actually calling him an idiot in her head. "I'm British," she added defiantly.

"No, no, no. Which African country are you from?" he asked persistently. "You look... Ugandan or something..."

He was starting to test Rachel's patience; she could feel herself tensing up. She sighed and replied slowly, as she always did when in this situation, "My parents are actually from Jamaica, not 'Uganda or something'. But I was born in London, so I'm Br..."

But her explanation was wasted. He completely disregarded most of what she said and honed in on one thing.

"– Ah Jamaica – Bob Marley, *ja*? I like Jamaica, it's cool. I don't like people from Africa."

Rachel was just about to let some *patois* loose on this fool, when she heard someone else ask: "And where are you from?"

This man's voice was deeper than the checkered-shirt man's voice. You could tell that he was Austrian, but he had obviously been to an international school as his English had a slight American twang to it. He had short dark brown curly hair with hazel eyes. He was wearing jeans and a grey T-shirt, which sho-wed his athletic body. His eyes connected with Rachel's and he winked at her.

"I'm from Upper Austria," Checkered-Shirt answered proudly. His emphasis on the word "upper" caused the pitch of his voice to rise to an awkward level.

"I bet you're from Fucking, aren't you?" said another man with a slightly husky voice. Rachel didn't even notice him at first, as she had been staring at the 'fake American'. This new guy had really short, straight dark brown hair, and intensely green eyes. He was also wearing jeans, but donned a white T-shirt and had a slightly slimmer physique. He was taller than the 'fake American'.

Checkered-Shirt struggled to respond and looked flustered. "Well… you know that –"

"– You are, aren't you?" said Fake-American, laughing.

"Are you from *Unterfucking*?" Husky teased.

"No. He must be from *Oberfucking*," answered Fake-American.

"Actually, I think you're right – look at him," said Husky. By now Checkered-Shirt was clearly feeling uncomfortable. The two men laughed some more, while Rachel smiled on in glee.

"Ok, so why don't you just fuck off now, ok?" said Fake-American, and then both men guided Rachel away to another area of the corridor.

"Phew, thank you! That guy was really fucking annoying me – get it?" said Rachel as she giggled to herself and was half expecting her new-found friends to join in. Her laughter was met with an awkward silence.

"I'm sorry, British people aren't allowed to tell that joke to us Austrians," Fake-American said, in a very serious tone. "It's highly offensive."

"No, she's not British, remember, she's Jamaican!" Husky responded. The friends looked at each other and then laughed once more.

"Ha! Very funny – not," she said, trying hard to conceal the biggest grin on her face.

"Sorry, Jamaica," said Husky.

Rachel gave him a disapproving look. "Look, my name is Rachel, ok?" she insisted.

"Ok, Rachel. Well My name is Felix," he replied. "And this," he added pointing at Fake-American, "is Tobias." Tobias. She liked that name.

"Well, nice to meet you both… I think," said Rachel. She paused and squinted at the two men in front of her in an attempt to read their characters. She eventually smiled. "Right, show me a good place to go out, please."

They laughed, they drank, they danced. This was the first time that she felt really comfortable since she'd been in Vienna. They took her under their wings as they showed her around the city and informed her of various Austrian customs. They became very close over time, and she valued the input that they had in her life.

She was struggling to understand Austrian-German. Whenever somebody spoke to her in that language, her usual response would be to smile and nod and say "*Ja*" every now and then. So Tobias pushed her to speak German. They agreed to meet for couple of hours each day to just talk. Rachel thought that he was a tough teacher and felt that he was a little impatient with her whenever she got anything wrong. She was convinced that there was a flaw in his teaching method, but really she just she didn't like anyone telling her what to do. Despite these occasional minor tiffs, they enjoyed each other's company and he made her laugh a lot.

Felix had the same political theory lecture as her. They hung out at a coffee shop opposite the university for an hour or two after the lecture to discuss what had been taught. They bonded over *Lattes* and Baileys hot chocolates as their conversations went beyond what happened at university.

"Rachel, I –," said Felix one day as Rachel talked about some family problems back home. He had clasped her hand in his and coughed to clear his throat. As he caressed her hand, he said: "Let me start again," he said as he chuckled to himself. "Look, if there's anything you need, anything at all, just let me know; I'm here for you. Ok Jamaica?" he said with a smile. Rachel smiled back. She felt close to Felix but she was unsure about her feelings towards him.

'…What if I…' mused Rachel, and then a screech from a nearby cat brought her out of her reverie.

Rachel felt nauseous again and closed her eyes. This time her memory took her back to the morning the three of them found themselves on Felix's balcony in the corridor's dining area watching the sunrise.

They had reminisced about the good times they had had during last night's escapades, but now they were silent. Rachel listened to the birds singing as Felix fell asleep. Tobias quietly admired her dark brown, medium length afro-textured hair as the soft morning sunrays touched it. He stared at her full luscious lips as they glistened in the light. From the corner of her eye, Rachel saw that Tobias was starting to move his hand towards hers. She felt a spark as his fingers touched her skin, and breathed in sharply. They slowly caressed each other's hands, playing, stroking, teasing… Then they turned in to look at each other. She noticed a glint in his eyes. He pulled her hand in towards his face and he gently kissed it. Their faces moved closer towards each other until they could feel each other's warm breath regularly against the others skin; their chests were rising and falling faster and faster as their breathing got heavier. Their noses encircled each other, around and around while Rachel's hand gently stroked his face and then pulled him in closer until they finally kissed.

After a while, they had left the balcony and slowly made their way through the front door, hand-in-hand, to go to Rachel's room a few floors below.

"Good morning, guys – see you later," Felix yawned.

"Good morning, Felix. *Schlaf gut*," Rachel had whispered

"I hope you guys sleep well," he replied. She noticed that his smile was a little more strained than usual and felt a pang of sadness, but quickly brushed it aside and put it down to his tiredness.

Pfeilgasse. Rachel opened her eyes again and looked at the building. She could still locate where her bedroom had been. It now looked dormant in the darkness. She dragged herself further down the street and crossed over to the other side. After a few minutes she came to a little park. She remembered that this was where she thought an elderly woman had aggressively shouted abuse at her, only to find out later that it was in actual fact a greeting. At the time, she didn't really know how to react to an altogether much too enthusiastic, rough sounding: "*Grüß Gott!*" She was just shocked. That was her first encounter with 'strange' Austrian customs.

This park was also the location of her first snow fight in Austria. There had been a lot of shouting, rolling about and frolicking on the frozen ground, carpeted with something resembling white velvet. She was with a larger group of friends this time, but of course, Tobias and Felix were also there. She ended up with the flu for a few days. Felix came by quite often to keep her company. When she insisted that he should go out and enjoy himself, he replied in a mock-serious tone: "Jamaica, you are stuck with me. I'll always be there for you." They stared at each other and then they both burst into laughter.

'However Tobias was a joke,' thought Rachel. 'I mean, seriously, how hard is it to bring someone a clean spoon when they are sick so that they can take their medicine? Or to get all the items that are on a shopping list? Or to not get any fucking crumbs on the bed? Argh – he was so infuriating at times, he could never get anything right! I felt like I was the adult in the relationship! At times, I couldn't honestly say that I loved him. I'm glad to be rid of him! But… I miss him…'

A bitterly cold breeze quickly brought her back to reality. 'How did I end up here? Why did he do this? I thought he loved me?' She felt so alone, even though people were walking past, laughing, happy and openly affectionate '…but if he loved me then he wouldn't have done this to me…' She wanted to get away as quickly as possible. She ran.

She found herself on the main road that led to Schottentor station; the station where a few months earlier she had made a fool out of herself, crying in pain as she searched Tobias' eyes one last time for a clue as to why he was doing this; to find out if this was just one of his 'jokes' again. But there had been no hint of a smile in his eyes; just suffering. She felt conflicted. She had wrapped her arms around him one last time, but he stood frozen like a statue. In the moment he had begun to disentangle his body from hers, she had pushed him away and darted towards the escalator. As she started to descend, she turned to see his face, but he was already walking out of her life; his body disappeared from her view. His final words still echoed in her ears… "I will always love you, Rachel," he whispered, "but I can't stand you trying to fix me anymore. I am not broken..." It sounded so obvious and effortless when he said it like that. But he had just stabbed her in the heart.

This same feeling now erupted again from inside of her – she vomited again. "Are you ok?" asked one concerned passer-by. This question triggered a river of tears to stream down her face. "No! I'm not ok!" she wanted to scream, but instead she ran off. The cold wind felt like daggers against her skin, but she didn't care; in fact, she welcomed the pain and wanted more of it. She kept on running until she could not run any longer. She then slumped to the ground, curled up into a ball and gently cradled herself to sleep between sobs of tears.

"Hey Jamaica!" she heard a husky voice exclaim. She dozily looked up. Directly in front of her she recognized those green eyes instantly. They were not full of pity; they were radiant with love. Felix was crouching down in front of her.

"It's so nice of you to drop by my flat, and I know you've been stalking me and everything. But you know, you don't need to hide outside anymore...Why don't you come inside this once, so that you can get warm, ok?" said Felix. He smiled, got up and stretched out an open palm towards her...

Lichterfelde Blues

Clementine Burnley

It is ten in the morning. Sunday in West Berlin means no shopping and lying to my father on the telephone about going to church. Last night, searching frantically for bus fare in an old handbag, I found the little green membership card with my name, denomination and year of baptism. It is wrinkled and faded; the last entry dates back to lower secondary school. Turning it over in my hands, I looked at the neat columns of numbers and signatures. Each month I had paid 500 Central African francs in church fees. The sums were written in a careful, childish hand, Esango's expression was always approving as he handed it back to me. At the beginning, faith was simple. Now I am less certain.

I have not been to chapel for a long time. I stopped paying church fees myself the year I left home. My father carried on. He pretended I would find another house of worship that would be glad to see I had belonged to a traditional congregation. Fifteen years later, I have not yet found a new church. What I lack is conviction.

There is no shortage of poorly heated buildings, with services attended by elderly, earnest people. Round the corner from my flat there are café-style gatherings for young urban believers. There are frothy hot drinks and leaflets, men with braided goatees and girls draped with floral scarves. With their friendly stares, they seem a little too pleased to see me. It is not my sort of thing.

I do not know how to explain to Pa the discomfort I feel hesitating at these entryways to foreign doctrine: at the light-coloured eyes pulling me in, at the pink lips mouthing unfamiliar words. There is no singing. The indecipherable sounds the people make are unsettling enough to overcome whatever impulse brought me in. I push out onto the street and stand for a brief moment.

I was baptized underwater at the bend of the Jengele River to a chorus of song that lifted me out of the gentle current. Since then, the clear confidence that took me into the river has dribbled away, much like the drops of water that trickled down my legs and onto the low-cut stubble of elephant grass on the bank.

Pa is ready for me to go Quaker, Episcopalian, anything short of the dancing and drumming of the prosperity gospel that has invaded his community. Behind the dark glasses he has taken to wearing in church, he rolls his eyes at the naked manipulation and the bartering of worship for personal gain. Despite his objections, there is no thought of a life outside the fold. Everyone goes. The Sunday service is as much a part of normality as going to school in

Down Beach or shopping at the crowded New Town market for bunches of curved green plantains and freshly cleaned cow belly.

I remind myself to call home, as I do every week. Pa will wait for the phone to ring, sitting in his cane chair with the newspaper, snorting at the spelling errors. My call is timed to catch him after his nap and before he goes to talk politics in his men's club. Pa will dangle his legs comfortably from an old leather-and-aluminium-framed bar stool and eat boiled peanuts while explaining why the government has no hope of reversing the decline of standards in the civil service. His friends will nod and reply as if they have not heard this all before.

We have woken up late, for me, but still too early for Idris. Living in Berlin on and off for the last ten years, I have grown attached to its oddness. This wannabe city is really a collection of sprawling villages with ambition. Lichterfelde is a quiet place on the outskirts of the urban core. I look after a house here when the owners are away. There are long avenues flanked by red-leafed chestnuts, oak and elm. The pavements are wide enough for large prams and small vehicles.

People move to Lichterfelde for space and security. Not that anywhere in Berlin is unsafe, as cities go. Still, commuters can park expensive cars here overnight without fear. Elsewhere, drivers of cars with long names like Mercedes Benz or BMW might find charred wrecks greeting the daylight with skeletal metal bones, slow-burning barbecue fuel having found its way into the unguarded chassis. I do not drive but used to have a bike before it was stolen. I remember the feeling of unreality, facing the spot where it used to be chained to the railing.

I am out of kilter with the world around me. Sitting down after six o clock in the evening is not an option. By eight most nights I am nodding and pretending to keep up with the conversation. I would rather stay awake like other human beings. So I come to Lichterfelde to sit in the sun when it is there. When the sun is not out, I sit in the cold light that leaks reluctantly from the clouds. I come to Lichterfelde for the garden. An enclosed outdoor space is useful in the afternoons, when I bare my skin to the sun. Light resets the clock in my cells that sends me to sleep when the grownup part of the day begins.

In summer I leave the doors open and sit in the garden with a book. Even in eastern Germany, it is sometimes summer for a month or two. Everyone sits outside, so I look normal. In winter I look under-dressed but there are few here to notice. In the garden, there is no one to watch me shiver and count down the minutes until I can go indoors. The heating in the dining room stopped working months ago. So when I go back inside it usually takes me a long time to warm up. When it rains or snows I do not bother to keep a circadian rhythm and go to bed early instead.

I come to Lichterfelde mostly to write and to get away from complications. This time I have brought Idris with me, which makes little sense. His being here is not simple. When I am alone I follow a set routine. In the mornings I open the windows, dust the gleaming furniture, water the plants on each floor. I keep one palm on the banisters as I go up and down the stairs. The painted wood is slick to the touch.

I write seven pages – sometimes more, never less. I gaze through the bars on the windows. The thick metal bars are there to keep intruders out and possessions in. I have lunch: tinned ravioli or a bowl of sweetened tapioca in milk, with ice and oven-roasted peanuts. In the afternoons I sit outside on the half-wall that encloses the lawn and stare at the trees. It is always clean and tidy inside the house. I make believe it is mine, this beautiful middle-class home. It is full of books I have not read, nor will ever read. They are mostly in German, which I understand. But I no longer read so that I can tell people I have read this one or that one when they ask. For purely social purposes, it's usually enough to know the title. Few people care what's inside a book of over one hundred pages. There are film versions of all works deserving of mention over dinner.

When I was younger I planned to read all the books that were important and then, halfway through my life, read them all again. All those words would fill me up and I would overflow with brilliance. Understanding, like religious belief, would manifest in inspired action. It did not. I have swallowed and spat up enough facts to realize that the consumption of information is insufficient. If I started to re-read all the books I have already read, I would die before the last page of the last book was turned, which would be fairly pointless. It's hard to tell which ones would be important enough to re-read or when I will reach my halfway point. That's why I write instead.

It is the middle of November. Summer is more mirage than memory. The wide pavements are invisible through dirty ice. Afraid of falling, many older people have stayed indoors this winter. Others have attached awkward-looking metal hooks to the bottoms of their shoes. All but a few have given up on scraping at the hard surfaces to make a safe path for walking. The occasional spray of grit lies on the slippery ice like confetti, more ceremonial than functional.

Idris and I arrived late last night. I waited until morning to turn up the thermostat in the musty, creepy cellar, so the house is cold. Outside, a few fiery leaves cling stubbornly to the beeches. I can see them through the bars on the windows as I walk back and forth between kitchen and dining room. Idris is half-asleep in the shower. He is not good in the morning so I am preparing breakfast on my own. By early afternoon, his libido will come into alignment with mine and we will go back to bed.

Children squeal and run outside, scattering the mounds of snow that are piled up outside the house opposite. A shovel is propped up against the garage wall. Perhaps the shoveller is sitting on the toilet inside, cursing the weather and children, or thinking of deserts, rock gardens and hot springs. A thin yellow dog is spinning in circles, snapping at its own tail. It is lost in the chase, dizzy with speed, surprised when its teeth close on its intended target. The high-pitched yelping reaches me as it lets go of its tail. The dog shakes its head, tongue lolling pink, then returns to its dreams of flying. I laugh and fancy it knows I am spying.

Idris is still not downstairs. He is a night owl, just starting to perk up at five in the evening. He is at his most animated by midnight when I am fast asleep. So of course he takes a long time in the morning. Idris thinks of me as rooted, authentic in a way that he is not. This is ironic. I am in Berlin because here there is no pretence of belonging. I have never stood in the shadow of the Wall. Authentic Berliners knew it as more than lumps of graffiti-smeared tourist memorabilia.

Last night I had fallen asleep on Idris' side of the bed on purpose, waiting for him to come upstairs. He had picked me up off the mattress, tucking me under the covers as he settled: a firm kiss, a leg stretched over mine, an arm to pin me down and he was snoring. I lay awake a long time, feeling my foot fill up with a numbed prickliness. It took me a long time to untangle and rub some feeling back into the limb. By then I was wide-awake again and mildly annoyed.

His unobtrusive presence had filled the Internet café where I had gone to look for a calling card. I had fumbled and peered without my glasses until he handed me a plastic card with a photograph of brightly dressed people holding up mobile phones and smiling. I had looked at his hands, steady and brown. They looked safe. He had noticed me staring. Embarrassed but determined, I had struck up a conversation that led to a drink in the café around the corner.

When Idris is in Berlin with me he listens to music and draws the black and white comic strips from which he is making a very good living this month. He is trained as a pipeline draughtsman. He was head of a team of three in Hamburg the autumn I met him. At some stage, Idris had perfected the art of looking as though he enjoyed reproducing the monotonous detail of power stations and refineries, enough to convince a series of employers. He cannot do that so well any more since he began to draw graphic novels. I would like to return to the places he draws. The constant pretence required for Idris to do his job has started to wear on him. So he is on sick leave and, in my opinion, unlikely ever to go back to his draughtsmanship or to Friedrich, Georg and Horst in Hamburg.

The dining table looks decent: no sign of last night's hurried arrival, the plates put aside unwashed, stacked in a neat heap in the kitchen sink. I have cleared a space among the newspapers and books for myself and Idris to eat the morning meal: muesli, fruit, milk, juice, plain yoghurt – all organic. Idris only eats organic food. On my way to the train station to pick him up, I had stopped at my local organic supermarket for the first time since I moved to Lichterfelde. They sell hemp seed, which I was mildly surprised to find, is legal and healthy to eat.

After listening to Idris snore for a bit I had eased myself out from under his outstretched limbs and gone to the toilet downstairs. On the way back up, I had stopped on the landing, where the moon traced an outline of the window on the floorboards. I had been barefoot as usual indoors and my feet were cold. The stairwell is unheated. As usual for German houses, the heating is switched off at night. There had been a light on in the stairwell of the house next door. I had thought I could see the pale outline of a man through the glass.

I stood looking for a moment, feeling safe in the darkness that surrounded me. I had left the light off in case it woke me up completely. It's better to feel my way to the bathroom and back, slipping into bed and warming my feet against Idris' smooth calves. He never appears to notice me creep in and out. At intervals he reaches out to rearrange me against him in his sleep. This is comforting but not entirely satisfying.

I am finally falling asleep when I hear a rattling at the window – or is it at the door? I tell myself the house is settling. Every house makes strange noises at night. There is no one trying to get in. In the detective shows I watch, there is always a woman walking down a dark alley, looking over her shoulder. Her chin-length brown bob will swing wildly as she begins to run but we all know how that ends. The struggle is short. The police are there the next day, just in time to take notes. The woman lies, a silent witness to their cleverness. Her limbs are splayed, her dress revealing. The body is eventually covered up. The character dies before the introductory credits come on screen.

The real story is of a beefy detective with a dysfunctional personal life hunting down an irrational male killer. Television is a world filled with violence toward lone women. Girls who wear ankle-length skirts and go home with men do not run down alleys alone. But even with the calves of a full-grown man warming my feet, I am still nervous in this creaky house on the border of a post-communist state. Berlin is not yet irretrievably fixed in the West. In the memory of true Berliners, the city drifts back and forth between past and future.

I take the seeded wholemeal rolls out of the oven and call Idris to breakfast again. He calls back, a muffled series of sounds I do not understand. When I go upstairs, he is brushing his teeth in the shower with his back turned. His shoulder blades jut from his slender torso. His angel-wing tattoo is slick with water. Twin crescents of overlapping feathers outline his collarbone and trail down his back. It is new, about as old as his first graphic novel. Eventually his line manager will spot it and there will be a stiff conversation, at the end of which he will probably resign. If he moves to Berlin I will have to decide who I want to be. I am not the same when he is away and not sure I like what I am when he is around. It is hard work having a lover. A pet would agree with me more.

I go back downstairs and bring the foil bag with the white tea he prefers to the table. The water in the teapot is below boiling. I measure the temperature: seventy-six degrees Celsius. I drop the fuzzy white buds in and watch them unfold. Silver Needles are picked on only two days each spring. I myself, drink powdered black tea of unspecified origin. The difference in our food habits sends me on grocery-shopping safaris. I am lonely sometimes and find it is hard to catch the eyes of cashiers everywhere. They watch purses and security mirrors instead.

When Idris is not in town I shop at the Asian grocery. They have plantains and yams. At Lidl or Penny, I pick up whatever German food is on offer. The service at both is equally uninspired but the queues are anaemic and aisles wide. Lidl and Penny do not switch their merchandise around to confuse and manipulate their customers. The tins of preserved meals I eat are piled up in metal enclosures beside Christmas specials, glittery jogging suits and tree ornaments. There are fewer fresh ingredients, which suits me fine. Idris is a vegetarian. I am finding it hard to combine the unfamiliar vegetables he eats, into a meal.

I have been brought up to catch, gut and pluck animals. In Germany few people could tell where to take hold of the internal membranes of the animals they eat, to eviscerate without rupturing the gall bladder, spilling bitterness throughout the meat. I learned to do this well because if I did it badly, we had to eat the bitter-tasting meat anyway. Idris does not know this about me. Before he gave up eating animals Idris had never thought about what went on inside them before they arrived in the refrigerated section of the store. He gave a lot of thought to what happened to them and then he gave up eating meat. Still, he has not thought about the gall bladder and the taste of the yellow and black secretions it produces. It is not the sort of conversation I want to have with him.

I miss the open markets at home; the un-shuttered eyes of the women, the neat heaps of spices, beans and rice. The lighting in Lidl and Penny is soulless. It bleeds already pale skin tones, transforming people from beige-pink-grey to plain grey. I am brown-grey there. At the *Einkaufsgenossenschaftdeutscher-kolonialwarenhändler*, where I buy *Gut und günstig*, the lighting is better. It's pale yellow instead of harsh white fluorescent. When I look at myself in the mirrored surfaces of the cheese counter at Edeka, I seem less ashy. The skin on my face absorbs the yellow and throws it back out. My face looks warm and almost happy.

There is a customer service inspection at the stores every once in a while. If you happen to buy your food during the short interval when the inspectors are there, you will think you have been transported to a North American store complete with smiles and "have a nice day." I imagine the shifts are long and the conditions hard. Still, a forced politeness is more agreeable than *Schnauze ohne Herz*.

At the smaller organic shops the staff are sometimes pleasant; perhaps in the spirit of compassionate, cruelty-free shopping. So when the man at *Biogrande* asks me if I would like to join his membership programme and get twenty-five per cent off the price of my organic groceries I weigh up the human contact against the price and try to calculate how long this thing with Idris will last. Without a lover will I need kindness more, or less?

At the table Idris and I sip tea and eat rolls. I look at the chapter he finished drawing last night. There is a woman running down a dusty road, laughing. The woman looks confident, competent. She is alive.

I look up from my plate to see that a man I do not know is inside the house. I do not recognize him. Later on I find out that is his name: Hermann. I have not heard the key turn in the lock. Perhaps the door was open. Have I left the door open by accident? My mind is working slowly. It is ten in the morning. I am house-sitting with Idris. There is an older man inside the house with us.

I sit frozen as this powerfully built, bristle-haired man lumbers into the dining room. He is moving swiftly, with purpose. Toward me. He has not taken off his shoes.

I put down my roll. The butter and half-chewed bread form a sticky lump in my throat. I am struggling to understand what is happening. Hermann is unsmiling. I am smiling at him, shocked and wondering but smiling. All proprieties have been transgressed. He has not rung the old-fashioned metal bell that hangs beside the front door. In Texas I could shoot him without further ado and then call the police. If I were a blond cowgirl, that is. But in Berlin I am smiling and waiting for him to tell me why he is inside the house, ignoring my lover, who is after all a man younger and stronger than him. In Berlin I hesitate to call the police. Instead I wonder how to remove an intruder from a space that he has made unsafe.

Idris is watching me, his almond-shaped eyes calm. There is a small brown birthmark above his top lip. I will him to stay seated and contain his strength and protectiveness until they are really needed. In case Hermann decides to be afraid after all.

Hermann has been watching the house. He has seen me come and go and grown curious. So he has come in to see what I am doing there with Idris. His green felt jacket is a traditional Bavarian cut. He reminds me of a woodsman of the kind who lead small children deep into dense forests. Hermann is well dressed, in corduroy trousers and a wool cardigan. The buttons are brown and made of wood. They are carved into the shape of tortoises. Under the cardigan is a woven cotton shirt. His tweed cap is tucked forward over the papery skin of his forehead. There are liver spots on his fingers. I look at Hermann's hands while he is talking. The joints of his fingers are thickened, his ridged nails manicured.

Keine Angst vorm schwarzen Mann.

Hermann says this several times. There is a man coming to sweep the chimney. He is worried I will be afraid of the black man. But a man covered in soot is not one to be afraid of. Plus there is no soot in the chimney. Idris is far too health-conscious to ever light a fire and breathe in particulates. But I am afraid of Hermann's bullying certainty – how he walks in with no thought of asking permission, no obligation to announce that he is about to be present. No fear or need to tell me he is coming beforehand. Hermann allowed to be anywhere, to protect me from a black man who is coming to clean the chimney.

Can he see on my face that I am breathing carefully? I am watching him for any sudden moves. Perhaps he has a fixation. Where I come from there are no chimneys or chimney sweeps. The houses are open all day long. Windows and doors are only locked at night to keep out insects, snakes, and lovers. There are curtains in front of the open doorways so people can change their clothes without being seen from the street. A constant stream of people come and go, bringing stories, selling snacks, dropping off cooking ingredients and utensils. It is easier to drop by than to telephone. When people come calling they stop in front of the curtain and knock on the wall or on the doorframe. Everyone walks in and out but no one enters without announcing his or her presence.

Once a neighbour's wife, Mami Etta; had grown tired of her husband's violent bullying and come to hide in our front room. Mami Etta's husband was afraid of my mother and so he had stood by our front door and coughed. Papa Etta had coughed for an hour, stopping at intervals, going away and returning. He had not been invited to enter and so he had gone away again. Mami Etta had spent the night. Early the next morning my mother had taken her back home and talked to Papa Etta. My mother had mentioned the police and money he owed to the committee that manages the affairs of the neighbourhood, which is mostly collecting contributions for births and funerals. There had been no more trouble.

Anyway, chimney sweeps are lucky. I have seen the postcards in the second-hand shop on the High Street where I buy my clothes. Chimney sweeps are blond children who throw magic mushrooms and four-leaf clovers on the ground. This seems unlikely in a country that has rules for the direction in which parked cars should face on the street. Chimney sweeps also give lucky business cards to people. Used-car dealers in Berlin pay dark-skinned immigrants to tuck little cards with advertising into the window frames of parked cars. The cards often end up inside the window frame; trapped between the glass and the innards, they jam up the mechanism. Which is not lucky. I cannot see how Hermann and his chimney sweeps fit into my Sunday.

I think to myself:

"Hermann, did I ask you to protect me?"

"Did you break in to reassure me?"

A man in blackface is coming. Not today but soon. On Monday.

I would like to know:

"Hermann, are you afraid?"

"What have you come to see?"

I ask these questions in my head. It turns out Hermann lives next door and has a key for emergencies. My being was an emergency. The grotesque tale of a man covered in soot had come into Hermann's head on the way over to see me. I am unable to speak. Like the woman from the detective show, I am silent. Idris has not spoken at all but is standing up and walking towards the front door. Hermann is between him and the exit. Trailing in their wake, I watch Hermann twist his hand behind his body to reach the door handle and open the door without turning his back on Idris and I. He looks nonplussed as the door shuts in his face.

Winter in Europe

Noah Hofmann

It is winter in Europe. Finally. After months of meetings and presentations –
some in real life, some virtual, too many during the night… – After successful
and sometimes also failed projects my holidays have finally begun. Finally.
And finally I'm sitting in the bus to Winterberg, cuddled in my warmest
pullover. I'm looking out of the window and letting my senses rest. I bought
the beloved pullover at home and of course, it was utterly expensive. The
winter tourism industry of the East Ethiopian trading union is a near mo-
nopoly, reflected in the prices. And despite the expense, I still bought it at
home. I simply don't have the nerves to constantly negotiate with locals over
the price of products that, only a few hours later, tear due to lack of quality.
Not during my holidays.

The bus is full. The driver is a slender and airy person with carefully curled
but carelessly dyed black hair. Only the sporadic blonde beard stubbles on
zher chin suggest its original colour. It is hard to estimate zher age, since Europeans age differently. Zher skin already starts to hang over zher cheekbones,
exhausted from too many visits to tanning studios. In a few years probably
the criteria 'looks too old for tourist work' will also be the driver's destiny. I
estimate zher age to be about 29.

In fluent Kiswahili zhe introduced zhemself as Hans in a high and soft sounding voice when we entered the bus. A tourist group with a heavy Kilwan
accent sitting in front of us started an open debate about whether or not Hans
could be a Viking because of zher stature and facial features. When zhe finally
affirmed it one part of the group first couldn't believe zher, because zhe looked
too short and too slender for what zhey thought a real Viking would look like.
I had to put earphones in my ear. Zhey must have questioned zher for at least
half an hour. But now everybody seemed to be sleeping and I hear the driver
singing quietly. European languages consist of many strange sounding noises.
For example the combinations of 'st', 'sp' or the infamous 'ch' just sound kind
of aggressive. On the other hand I think zhey totally underline the European
nature. There seems to be something raw and untamed in everything.

The idyllic and white landscape flowed by like a wavy ocean of snow and ice.
I could not imagine such beauty on this cold continent, full of poverty, misery
and war. Like all bus routes, this route through central Europe led through
only selected areas that had achieved a certain level of development and
therefore looked presentable. When we entered the suburbs of the German
tourist Metropolis Winterberg we saw many traders on the street wrapped in

coats and blankets, warming zhemselves by burning trash cans. The sight had a rough charm, but when the air conditioning sucked the smell of frostbite and rottenness into our bus, one could only imagine what was happening behind this idyllic facade. To the locals, Europe's winter is like a merciless kraken spreading its deadly cold and snow white tentacles over the country, into the frozen maw of which countless white bodies disappear only to be spat out lifeless a few months later, covering the meadows with death and hopelessness in spring.

It is a raw continent full of contradictions. When the Songhai philosopher Adama Seydou Emegwali described the Europeans as dirty, instinct-driven and lazy 400 years ago, zheir spirit and zheir dances already had intrigued several Ethiopian discoverers. But until today, Europe struggles. The people are not yet aware. Europeans have not yet learned to participate in perhaps zheir only possible chance at progress: the business of winter tourism. I often pity zhem and at the end of the year I donate my few shillings to charity, not knowing if zhey ever reach zheir aim, but what more can I do?

"People who so desperately hold on to genderism will never fit into civilization." Tendaji must have read one of my thoughts while I was looking out of the window. "Zhey force people into social classes according to some very basic biological features between zheir legs or on zheir chests."

"This is a stereotype," I responded.

"Don't you dare to say that! You know it's true. Who if not I knows how desperately zhey hold on to zheir genderism and zheir rules of which gender is allowed to love which and so on..." zhe says. I look at Tendaji pointing at zher beard, suddenly remember and then laugh out loud. Zhe was right and I was ignorant. The first time we took our holidays in Europe zhe was drunk and totally intrigued by the long, flowing and wildly flapping European beard of a local. Tendaji simply couldn't stop playing with it. But when zher fingers slowly slid to the local's bottom the situation quickly deteriorated. I only remember the local's face turning red like a baboon's arse and zhem jumping off from Tendaji's chest and a druid waving with animal bones, casting evil spells on us. I pushed Tendaji out of teahouse before zhe had the chance to become intrigued by the druid's beard as well.

"But I though do think we should give zhem a chance. I don't think zhey are as stupid as we always claim."

"I don't think zhey are stupid. Zhey're just simple – not evil, but simple people, who do not worry about all the things we worry about all day. We actually could learn from zhem – to think less, feel more and just be happy with what we have." At this point one of the Kilwan tourists turned around and participated in our conversation.

"I don't think zhey're evil, but be honest, zhey are really poorly developed. We've tried so much, tried to give zhem aid and education but though until today zhey haven't managed to learn even a single one of the languages of the neighbouring tribes. This is something we simply can't imagine. We can't imagine growing up having learned less than five basic languages, and with five you're still poorly educated. I think Europeans are just different in intellectual things. I maybe wouldn't directly define it as poor, but different. How can you educate in a country in which only about 50 languages and a few dialects exist and not even those are properly spoken and standardised?" I kept silent. "There is a reason you don't find any remnants of architecture here, though zhey always had much better building materials here then we have in Ethiopia." The tourist turned around again.

I thought about whether I should speak about the genocides the discoverers, especially those from nations like SLW (*Shirikisho La Waswahili*), *Baherero* or *Songhai*, committed when zhey found all the copper, coal and oil in Europe; whether I should speak about the labour system, which was a reaction of the SLW administration in Germanland after several uprisings against mining companies and which had nothing to do with the free will of the locals but, rather, with punishment and slavery. Slavery – the word, which comes from "Slaw", a European people, formerly proud, but zheir name became the international standard word for subjection, inferiority and – well…. enslavement, slavery. On the other hand there is simply too little known about it. I partially doubt it myself sometimes, because Europeans wouldn't welcome us as submissively as zhey do if we hadn't brought an enormous amount of progress and help into zheir mountains. Often it is also hard to verify European stories, because zhey often come from very small-minded and unintelligent speakers, who mostly tend to exaggerate. Zhey still haven't understood that fundamental knowledge has to be bound to intelligent people. But well… what do I actually really know?

I decided to stay silent. Tendaji seems to make friends with the Kilwan tourist. I'm not sure whether this is a good thing. Zhey sometimes drink too much, and to be honest, some tourists can be very rude and ignorant. Some of zhem get drunk and then vandalize shops, beat up locals, scare the horses of the carriages or just pee around sacred tribal totems or places. A local European government was recently charged because tourists from Batswana burnt zhemselves while climbing some kind of sacred tree with burning candles – a somewhat spooky tradition celebrated every winter in Europe. Maybe zhey can also learn to take those kind of actions as critical feedback on zheir traditions.

The bus leaves the suburbs and enters Winterberg city. We pass small teahouses and restaurants with names like "Barbarian Bavarian" or "Wild Viking", statues with Emegwali zhimself or other Ethiopian generals having fought in Europe, Ethiopian tourists in front of a restaurant, drinking and partying in strange long red costumes, flapping red hats and wearing scary looking fake white beards or fake white wings. I think there is still much to understand about the pale history of this white continent.

However I am open minded, curious, and really looking forward to another two relaxing weeks full of nature and inspiring and exotic adventures down here.

Waste of Mist

WoMANtis RANDom

I was one of these children who had so-called "*Klingelhose*",
Pants that you get at night, pants with sensors.
I peed in my pants till I was 12 years old.
Back then, I did not know how to articulate.
But sometimes, I still echo to this feeling.

Nebelschwaden gehen auf die Reise,
Am Ende, zum Tag, eingetaucht in
purple-pink sunset, way up the hill.
We are sun sad
and we sunrise

However, I am still glocally located to the house of becoming.
All good things are 3, I personally experienced the binary.
The undriven mechanism of complex stories is woven in
micro-gigantic politics which I witness in the subway.
Although that has never been an unfamiliar story.
And whoever portrays me as macro-aggressive,
should become a witness to the shift of conversations that I spark.
Conversations that are presented as news on a screen –
Multiple conversations have been foreseen –
for ages without senseless rages.
I might want to emphasize that I did not leave my communities. I was moved.
Certainly by the violence and the injustice that is conducted by the blood
law of Eurocentric history.
Where is the margin
if it is imagined as the outline of any kind of shape?
Isn't the margin all around me?
I colour in every pattern that I see and I start usually at the margin.
And what do I know about colouring in.

The last time, I remember feeling *joyeuse* about colouring out was, when I was… young, I guess.

Waking up with wet pants meant to draw rainy clouds. A whole chart to fill. Every day of the week.

I recall that I failed as I admired to paint straight raindrops, umbrellas and fluffy clouds.

Winter means decoration, means poopy Lametta and lights to brighten the days to come. There is

finally no excuse to overdue the fabulousness of celebrating the seasons of change.

My chosen families.

This was the time where glitter was accessible in

masses and for cheap.

Lametta made every single object and subject

celebrate what we had. And

we came together, all kinds of feminists and

activists because we do not hibernate well.

A few moons ago, waft of mists were going on a journey.

One sister and 10 invoices to feed.

As I receive another memory, I wonder.

I do not want to get it twisted, so I listen.

Her voice circles my attention while the others

are driven by the weekly circumstances of a gentrifying city

that we BOTH live in.

Saturday.

One sister and 10 other voices.

There were no surprises

When her radiohead Collapsed

Into water draining blue mountains

Blue

As an outcome of

Overstimulation.
There were no surprises
When her summer job in
Fairylands
Collapsed into voices that her own
In her head
Separated as a person can be
Filled with over-stimulation

One hit, one day,
One life
Attached to another
One story
Attached to another

Mind versus politrix
Tix Tix Tricks Ticks
Mind of our own
Mindlessness is what we own alone.
This person has no memory anymore.
In fact, memory is the last thing that helps.
And there were no surprises
But a seed to acknowledge
Without doubt and attempt
To stop her words from
Constructing my programmed
Ideas of what it means
To memorize
Personally
Not being me
To see monsters
To know that
The voices that we own ARE REAL
But a life in one imagined reality

Destroys perhaps all the 'other' realities.
REALI-TIES
Doesn't reality tie?

And we daily become true.
Take breath in un-comfort.
So that we become more true to ourselves.
As rain is water. And water became rare,

Black lives matter is the slogan that moves all bodies but with a limited speed.
In my mind, I demonstrate by just adding to the slogan:
All black lives matter. I add, because I can.

I nearly disappeared in front of people
And they all knew and know. They wanted to become
Witness of what I smelled before their investigation began.

What makes me attached to a person?
What makes me attached to a belief?
Am I allowed to share my fiction with you?
Who am I to judge?
My body is held in constant crises
as a result of complex capitalist global politics.
HOWever – My body is my throne.
Don't get it twisted!
Every refuse and resistance towards my dancing and singing on the street
brings me closer to the stories
and bodies who commute on the non-bourgeois sidewalks.
While big trucks are threatening and pushing my body to the sidewalk,
While I learn to longboard. Ha!
Minus 20 Grad and I feel like celebrating even more this winter.
What do I really know about all the people who disappear on purpose?

I agree, winter is a pitch creepy if you live further North of East and West because nobody would think of "the South" – or?

Who are these souls?

And who are 'the others'– the ones who are prepared as well?

Slightly blow their candles or

Re-shift their locations?

But it requires air to do so.

And I am aware of the air

and its movement since

I took my first sip and

took my first breath.

It was cold by the time the oxygen was delivered.

Inhaling - while just … escaping the waste of mist that has been surrounding me.

Why do I assume winter has to be cold?

I moved glocally further North.

I am unaware of the favourable climate change.

I am aware of the global changes that have always been balanced by which poles?

This winter feels cold

As if somebody tried to

Blow the fucking candle out of me.

There is something magical to witness another light.

There is something special about

Witnessing the fire while the surrounding is embedded

in a snow storm.

And there is something surprising within the single momentum

of using air –

to be alive while –

waiting.

Nesting.

Breathing.

Sharing stories of lights in the wintertime.

Back to the Beginning:
Klingelhosen fulfils all kinds of purposes.
The shame and the silence
that followed for 18 years.
Over-dreaming is a failure
rewarded by loud sounds in my pants
during an age
where more people already
achieved access
to my gender

RIIIIIING RING, it's such a BIG Thing

The pressure that you could not hold – again. This was in the 1990s.
Right in between the transition from one regime to the next.
Although, the heteronormative cis-iety would argue otherwise –
I was supposed to release pressure. PUNK! *Punkt.*
I was one of the last DDR-Afro-German-European-Diasporic peoples who
was born on the other side of the wall. However -
I am still fluid as the water, air, and fire that I move in
on the soils that have been transitioned into
spaces of belongings
regulated by their purposes of all kinds
I still hesitate to write on walls that are not considered my own. Not that I
believe in property – but I
also do not believe in punishment for artists of all kinds. My skin became
my wall. My clothes
became my wall. I became the reason for creating walls. In fact, the walls are
breaking with every
brick that is thrown at me.
It is particularly cold this year.
And I am not able to celebrate, whatever my friends celebrate.
Because I sit alone with my fears. When inside becomes an outside experience.
Then outside becomes an inside conversation.

Public transportation can cause physical conversations.

It happened one week before Trans Day of Remembrance.

I remember that light became important.

And I remember, I became important.

But the silence is poking my neck.

It needs air to breath

And so I will continue to believe:

That every living being has a story to tell. Complex not complicated as it might appear. To quote

Mos Def "There is a way ay ay ay, no matter what they say".

What a wonderful day. What a wonderful world. Thank you Louis.

And back to the roots:

If you are worried 'bout them – baby, don't worry, you know that you got me.

This is in remembrance of all the Black, gender-variant, fluid (self-)healers, to all the feminine-identified peoples we have lost, we will have, and their beloved ones, to all the women who have been mistreated, killed, and are still being captured within cis-tems of oppressions, especially to Black/Indigenous Women in Canada.

Authors' Biographies

Clementine Burnley

Clementine Burnley was born and raised in Cameroon. Writing is something she came to quite late in life. Now she writes because she has to. Clementine is a proud mother to three reflective, questioning and politically engaged young women. She has worked as a (critical) development researcher and consultant for long periods in England, Italy and Germany. In both her work and life she continues to learn, from the active people around her, how to create joyfully within a destructive system. You can find Clementine on social media at:

http://africanblackstar.tumblr.com

https://ezibota.com/about/clementine-burnley/

Bino Byansi Byakuleka

Bino Byansi Byakuleka was born in 1979 in Kabale, Uganda. He is a textile artist and lives in Berlin. While he was at school he was active in the Orthodox Church in Uganda. He received his Diploma in Industrial Art and Design from the Buganda Royal Institute of Art and Technical Education in 2005. In 2007 he received a scholarship to study in Greece at the St. Arsenios Monastry and the School of Creative Art. In August 2010 he applied for asylum in Germany and lived for almost two years in the Lager in Breitenburg near Passau in Bavaria. In August 2012 he started a protest camp in Passau (Klostergartenpark). He mobilised the refugees in Bavaria to join the protest march to Berlin. In October 2012 he joined the refugee protest camp at Oranienplatz. He is a full-time human defender; his focus is on LGBTIQ rights and to change the German Asylum law. In 2013 he founded the African Refugees Union and started the campaign "We are Born Free, my right is your right" in 2014. The aim of this campaign is to improve the inclusion of refugees in German society.

Noah Hofmann

Noah Hofmann is a Black cis-man, born in 1985 in Switzerland and now studies Applied Computing in Berlin. He describes himself as neurodiverse and is a social media activist on Facebook and Blogger (Aioon on "Arriving In The Future"). Also he is a self-identified freethinker, distributor of Black knowledge, advocate of radical Black self-love, declared enemy of white supremacy and a semi-professional self-promoter on Facebook. "Winter in Europe" is his first publication.

Njideka Stephanie Iroh

Njideka Stephanie Iroh is a writer, artist and activist currently based in Vienna. Her poem *"Decolonising Fragments of Streams of Thought"* was published in *"Utopia of Alliances, Conditions of Impossibilities and the Vocabulary of Decoloniality"* (Löcker Verlag, Vienna 2013). In a combination of spoken word, performances and lectures she deals with topics such as language, power relations, decolonisation and empowerment. The basis of her work is formed by PAMOJA –The Movement of the Young African Diaspora in Austria and in cooperation with other local and global Black and migrant organisations. She is the co-director of the project "Bodies of Knowledge" which was awarded the SHIFT 2015 grant in Vienna, Austria.

Elsa M'Bala

Elsa M'bala was born 1988 in Yaoundé, Cameroon. Since 2009, she has been a member of the poetry and acoustic band Rising Thoughts, with whom she organized the tour, "Struggle of the African Woman for freedom" in Germany and Jamaica. In 2014, she co-edited and presented the 6th issue of the magazine for the mental state, *freier* at Dak'art, the biennial for contemporary African art in Senegal. She uses music, poetry and performance as media. M'bala has been collaborating with various visual artists to bring forth her artistic vision. In 2015 She was one of the winners of the lauréats *découverte* at the Goethe Institut Kamerun and was invited to the "Chale Wote" festival in Accra, Ghana. Between conversations, car horns and *Waldgeräusche*, she talks about her experiences as an African daughter, a returnee, and a black female artist. She currently lives in Cameroon.

Muriel Mben

Born in Cameroon, Muriel Mben has been living in Germany for five years. After her Bachelor of the Arts in Language and Communications, she has started a Master of the Arts in Cultural and Social Anthropology in Marburg. She loves writing. Her first short story entitled *"La dernière pluie"* was published in 2013 by a French editor.

Sharon Dodua Otoo

Sharon Dodua Otoo is a Black British mother, activist, author and editor of the English language book series "Witnessed". Her most recent publication is the German language novella *"Synchronicity"* (edition assemblage, 2014) which will appear in English at the end of 2015. Sharon's first novella *"the things i am thinking while smiling politely"* was published in English in 2012 and appeared in German as *"die dinge, die ich denke, während ich höflich lächele"* in 2013 (both also in edition assemblage). She lives, laughs and works in Berlin.

WoMANtís RANDom

WoMANtís RANDom is a Black Gender Gifted artist. They are a media-acrobat, street-musician, dancer, painter, using text based art to talk about complex NOT complicated politics from a feminist 4th WAVE perspective.

Tigist Helen Schmidt

Tigist Helen Schmidt is an actor, writer, filmmaker and activist. She appeared in various films and performed in collaboration with various multidisciplinary artists. Her first book *"GOURSHA"*, highlights Ethiopian and Eritrean artists and is to be released in the fall of 2015.

Monique Simpson

Monique Simpson was born and bred in the UK but is of Jamaican heritage. She studied BA (Hons) European Studies with German at Royal Holloway, University of London, and as part of her degree she lived and studied for a year in Vienna, Austria. This was when German truly came to life for her and she came to understand and fully appreciate Germanic culture. She has always loved to write in various different forms since she can remember. She also loves to travel and experience new cultures as a direct response to her time in Vienna. So she recently decided to leave her job as a journalist in London to do so. She is currently living and working in Mexico so that she can immerse herself in Latino culture. Insights into her experiences can be found here: www.areyouhavingabubble.wordpress.com

Acknowledgements

Clementine Burnley

I am thankful for three things: family, friends, and the community. "*Winter Shorts*" could not have come to be without a community of writers, careful readers, supporters and believers to whom I say a very sincere "Thank you". In Bakweri I say "*Na somi saisai*" to Sharon, for believing in me before I was sure; my mother Gwendoline Etondi Burnley nee Martin who knew from the beginning, my father Robert Efesoa Gotthilf Burnley whose love was all-encompassing, my six siblings who taught me most of what I know, my cousins who are my siblings, my friends who are my cousins. My large ubuntu – Steinbergers, Burnleys, Martins, Brandts, Simei Kronert Che, USCUMA e.V qi gong group, Kwanzaa peepul and Phoenix e.V.

Sharon Dodua Otoo

Thank you dear writers for sharing your stories with us: the journey has been long and sometimes scary but always worth it. Thank you dear copy-editors and proofreaders, especially you dear Bartosz, for your watchful eyes and skilful pens (metaphorically speaking!). Thank you dear Jens for the layout and last minute corrections! Thank you Willi, Carina and Markus, as always, for your solidarity. Thank you once again dear Sita for your beautiful artwork.

Special thanks to Clementine for saving "*Winter Shorts*" from a dusty pile of good ideas and also for always saving me from myself; special thanks to Bino for saving Europe from the Europeans... and extra special thanks to Lewis for the cups of tea, "vegan" M&Ms and random stories that have no punchline.

The WiTneSSeD - Series

Sandrine Micossé-Aikins / Sharon
Dodua Otoo (Hg.)

The Little Book of Big Visions

How to Be an Artist and
Revolutionize the World

158 Seiten, 14.80 Euro
ISBN 978-3-942885-31-7

Olumide Popoola

Also by Mail

96 Seiten, 9.80 Euro
ISBN 978-3-942885-38-6

Nzitu Mawakha

Daima

Portraitband

96 Seiten, 123 Fotographien
19.80 Euro
ISBN 978-3-942885-48-5

Amy Evans

The Most Unsatisfied Town

96 Seiten, 9.80 EUR
ISBN 978-3-942885-76-8

*Alle Titel sind in Ihrer Buchhandlung erhältlich oder können direkt beim Verlag
bestellt werden:*

edition-assemblage.de